In the name of Allah,
the Most Gracious, the Most Merciful

Also by

Hedaya Hartford and Ashraf Muneeb

Your Islamic Marriage Contract

Birgivi's Manual Interpreted:
Complete Fiqh of Menstruation & Related Issues

IN ARABIC

ذكر المتأهلين والنساء في تعريف الأطهار والدماء
للإمام محمد بير علي البركوي (تحقيق)

منهل الواردين من بحار الفيض على ذكر المتأهلين في مسائل الحيض
للعلامة ابن عابدين (تحقيق)

إرشاد المكلفين إلى دقائق ذكر المتأهلين (تأليف)

Initiating and Upholding an

Islamic

Marriage

NEW REVISED EDITION

HEDAYA HARTFORD

AL-FATH
Research & publishing

Third Edition
(1428ah/2007ce)
Dar Al-Fath
P.O. Box 183479
Amman 11118 Jordan
Tel: (00962) 777 925 467   Fax: (009626) 515 6201
E-mail: info@alfathonline.com
Website: www.alfathonline.com

Library of Congress Cataloging-in-Publications Data

Hartford, Hedaya.
Islamic Marriage / Hedaya Hartford.
p. cm.
ISBN 978-9957-23-063-0 (alk. paper)

Cover design by Dar al-Fath
Book design and typography by the author

Contents

Preface

In the name of Allah, the Most Merciful, the Most Compassionate. Praise to Allah, Lord of the Worlds. Praise to Him who guides us to Islam. And blessings and peace upon our beloved Prophet Muhammad, the exemplar of the righteous, and upon his family and Companions one and all, those who followed after them, and all the righteous.

I ask Allah Mighty and Majestic to make this work purely for His sake and to reward out of His generosity those who have taught me, those who have helped in editing and producing this work, and those who read it.

May Allah increase the love, mercy and understanding between each Muslim husband and wife, and bless each Muslim with an increase of the love of Allah and His Messenger, Allah bless him and give him peace, in this world and the next. May Allah Most Generous honor us with obedience and may we not disgrace ourselves with disobedience. Ameen.

Praise to Allah, Lord of the Worlds. If I have been successful in this work, it is from Allah's generosity; and if I have made mistakes, it is because of my weakness and lack of knowledge. I ask Allah Most Benevolent to guide and protect me for He takes the hand of those who rely on Him.

This edition has been revised with some new additions as well as a few corrections. I have found while teaching this text that most readers breeze through and enjoy it without earnestly contemplating the subject matter. It is important to remember while reading this book that each point requires careful and deliberate reflection so as to fully understand its significance. It is essential that you ponder upon and then apply that which is personally relevant to you.

I have used the standard transliterations for Arabic supplications with the following exceptions:

h̲ for ح; kh for خ; s̲ for ص; t̲ for ط; ' for أ; ' for ع;

gh for غ; and dh for ذ.

If the reader finds any mistakes, please inform me so they can be corrected for further editions. Write to:

amedits@gmail.com

or

P.O. Box 963642
Sports City, 11196
Amman, Jordan.

Jumada al 'Ula 18, 1428/ June 3, 2007
Amman, Jordan

Our beloved Prophet,
Allah bless him and give him peace, said,

We have not seen anything better than marriage
for those who are in love

(Ibn Majah, 1847)

Marriage and faith have existed since the time
of the Prophet Adam, peace be upon him,
and will continue in the Hereafter

Ibn 'Abidin

1

Introduction

Worship Allah Mighty and Majestic
through marriage

In the name of Allah
Most Merciful and Most Compassionate

*I*SLAM IS A RELIGION that encompasses our lives in many aspects and on many levels, weaving a web among the various facets of our life. Among these is marriage. This book is written especially for those Muslims, who have recently embraced Islam and ethnic Muslims raised or living in the West, who have not yet married but are thinking to marry. Some chapters will be of interest to those already married as well. It is offered as a guide for preparing yourself to enter an Islamic marriage in spirit and form, as worship to Allah Mighty and Majestic. Themes found in this book range from practical and legal considerations, to spiritual concepts and perspectives, to the recognition of the new outlook and aspiration of Islam in your life. Lastly, this book is intended to make you aware of the responsibilities you are about to undertake through marriage in view of what Allah has demanded of you.

Invested with the khilafa (vice-regency) of creation, human beings are created in pairs, male and female. Marriage brings together individual Muslims, male and female, and forms the foundation of a successful Islamic society based on mutual rights and duties as well as the perpetuation of humanity. Allah Almighty says: "O mankind, fear your Lord, who created you from a single soul, and created its mate, and from the pair of them scattered countless men and women ... verily Allah ever watches over you" (Qur'an, 4:1).

Islam promotes the worship of Allah, the purpose of our existence, from the individual, to the familial, to the societal level. "I have not created jinn and mankind except to worship Me" (Qur'an, 51:56). By means of noble intentions, we transform our daily life into worship. As a primary decision in life, marriage, even more so, demands an appropriate intention; it should be made with the purpose of upholding the Prophetic example, drawing nearer to Allah, obeying Him and fulfilling the rights He has prescribed. You should also intend to preserve modesty, seek offspring and find companionship.

As well as these noble intentions, there must be a constant awareness in marriage whether the responsibilities required of each spouse are being done in a manner that pleases Allah Mighty and Majestic or in a manner that displeases Him. The ability and willingness of one to perform these responsibilities wholeheartedly should be kept in mind when contemplating marriage.

Surely you do not want to live a daily life of disobedience by discharging the obligations inadequately or by neglecting the duties you have brought upon yourself through marriage, thereupon invoking the displeasure of Allah Mighty and Majestic.

Righteous behavior is something between the individual and Allah Almighty. Righteousness is sought from all Muslims. Allah demands it, and it is expected of you.

Imam Sha'rani, in considering the importance of marriage, said in his *al-'Uhud al-Muhammadiyya*: "My brother, look to the Prophet Moses (peace be upon him) in renting himself for ten years in order to pay his mahr (marriage payment) and then you will realize the greatness of marriage."

In response to questions about mut'a (temporary marriage), the answer is that it is invalid and haram (unlawful) (*Sharh al-Ahkam al-Shar'iyya*). The popular misunderstanding or misinterpretation about the permissibility of temporary marriage comes from those who misinterpret hadiths; they construe a hadith while not knowing its legal standing, ruling or both.

Hadiths that permitted temporary marriage were abrogated by later hadiths. The following are but two among many of the superseding hadiths on this topic: Al-Hasan ibn Muhammad reported that his grandfather 'Ali ibn Abi Talib (may Allah be pleased with them both) said that the Messenger of Allah, Allah bless him and give him peace, prohibited temporary marriage in the year of Khaybar [for the first time] (Bukhari, 5523). Thereafter, during the conquest of Mecca, it was made halal (lawful) for three days, after which its prohibition was finalized, when the Messenger of Allah, Allah bless him and give him peace, said: "Verily it [temporary marriage] is haram (unlawful) from this day of yours until the Day of Judgment" (Muslim, 1406). This is a clear example of why we take legal rulings from the scholars of Sacred Law, and not from random hadiths.

The First Steps

THE MESSENGER OF ALLAH, Allah bless him and give him peace, said: "Verily this religion is inexorable, so enter its depth gently (Ahmad, 12618); if you try to seize it all at once it will overpower you" (Bukhari, 39). We must take this religion one step at a time. It is a complete way of life and requires time to adjust. In learning your religion, you must begin to re-examine and regard things in its new light. Apply Allah's commands in the spirit of 'We hear and we obey' (Qur'an, 5:7). Assimilating what you learn consistently will facilitate this. It is through Allah's mercy and wisdom that we are shown our faults gradually. As many converts to Islam can attest, it may take years to really shed non-Islamic manners and patterns of behavior. Whether new to Islam or not, your keeping to Islam is a tremendous blessing from Allah Most Beneficent, for in it lies the means to earthly and eternal happiness.

If you share this book with your spouse or prospective spouse, it is recommended that you highlight the parts most relevant to your situation. If you are a bit shy this might help in opening up a subject that you feel needs to be discussed.

If you want an untroubled marriage, it is important that you consider those matters that interest you, as well as those related to a particular fault you may have in order to change and overcome it. This could aid each of you in attaining those desirable responses and behavior patterns that promote a happy Islamic marriage. It should encourage and help you see the need for ridding yourself of those actions that are undesirable. It is easy to get married; the challenge is to see it through and make it a success.

Keep in mind that blessings often first appear as disappointments. Find counsel in the words of Allah Most Generous: "And it is possible that you hate a thing which is good for you and that you love a thing which is bad for you. And Allah knows and you know not" (Qur'an, 2:216).

Marriage and the New Muslim

$\mathcal{F}$OR NEW MUSLIMS, it is advisable to wait at least a year before considering marriage. Your new situation poses enough challenges without needing to make such a crucial decision. Consider for a moment how your views of life were before you really knew Islam. Consider how those views have changed and consider how much your views will change after entering Islam's depths. Marriage also tends to stabilize and set the social aspects and identity of your life. The direction you are moving in your life and how you identify yourself will be much harder to change once married. As a new Muslim with a rapidly changing outlook, the spouse you accept today might not be acceptable to you after some years of seriously practicing Islam.

Do not spend the first year looking for your future spouse; rather, give yourself the time and space you will need to learn and live Islam. Well-meaning people might insist or pester you to marry without delay; ignore their advice and pressure. Some believe that marriage will help you remain a Muslim—but marrying the wrong person can do just the opposite. A serious Muslim is not likely to leap into a marriage with a new convert simply because there are many variables and too much at risk. A religious Muslim would want to make sure that their potential spouse has the same dedication to and application of Islam. So who is this person they want you to marry? Often, they encourage you to marry someone you yourself would not accept after a year or two of learning and practicing Islam. There are exceptions to this, but the exceptions are few and far between.

If you are a student, you need to consider your priorities. Being a student at university often means that you find yourself on your own and alone for the first time. Accepting Islam may also mean that many of your friends have abandoned you, compounding this sense of loneliness. Marriage is often wrongly seen as a way to instantly create an island of comfort and companionship. In reality, marriage requires a great deal of responsibility, both financial and emotional. For this reason, Imam Abu Hanifa recommended that students of sacred knowledge not marry until they finish their (foundational) studies, because they easily get distracted if busy with earning a living or taking care of family duties.

The Prophet, Allah bless him and give him peace, said: "He who overloads his carriage neither reaches his destination nor keeps his carriage" (al-Jami' al-Saghir, 2524).

Who Should Marry

*A*FTER ESTABLISHING a firm base in your religion, you can begin to look at the legal aspects of marriage. These apply to both men and women, though the concerns of financial obligation lie entirely upon the man since he is responsible for the support of his family. The following list is taken from the *Book of Marriage* by Ibn 'Abidin's Radd al-Muhtar, an important fiqh (Islamic jurisprudence) reference. He summarizes that marriage is:

- Fard (obligatory) for someone who fears for his or her chastity.

- Wajib (requisite) for someone whose desire is overwhelming.

- Sunna (recommended) for a male who has the ability to have sexual intercourse, pay the mahr (marriage payment) and maintain a wife; and for a female who has the ability to fulfill the duties of a wife.

- Makruh (disliked) for someone who fears he or she will be unjust to a spouse.

- Haram (forbidden) for someone who is sure he or she will be unjust to a spouse.

These legal qualifications are not a mere checklist to determine whether you should marry or not. If you are in the disliked (makruh) or forbidden (haram) categories, then you need to improve yourself before considering marriage—you do not want to live a daily life of constant disobedience. If you know you will be unjust to your spouse, examine the reasons behind this and correct it according to Islam. This is part of our jihad al-nafs (spiritual struggle) in Islam.

If your desires are overwhelming but you feel you will be unjust to your spouse, the concern of being unjust supersedes the advice to marry. You should remain unmarried since the sin of oppressing a servant of Allah is more heinous than harming yourself.

Important worldly considerations include the ability to pay the marriage payment and support your wife. If you find yourself in an environment that is not conducive to God-fearingness and your desires are overwhelming, carefully emulate pious behavior. Secular societies are filled with sexual images and undertones; even if you do not directly acknowledge them, they influence your mind and spiritual state. Making a conscious effort to avoid the haram as well as to increase other aspects of your worship, such as fasting, will help you face the challenges of living in an un-Islamic environment.

Allah Most High says: "Marry those among you who are single... If they are in poverty, Allah will give them means out of His bounty; Allah is All-embracing, All-knowing. Let those who find not the means to marry keep themselves chaste, until Allah gives them means out of His bounty" (Qur'an 24:32-3).

The Messenger of Allah, Allah bless him and give him peace, advises: "Whosoever is able should marry, for it lowers the gaze and protects the private parts and whosoever is unable should fast for it is a protection" (Bukhari, 1905). Here 'able' means financially. Aside from this financial ability, a competent level of maturity and emotional stability are equally essential for both the man and woman.

2

Finding a Spouse

Forethought, not passion

Our beloved Prophet,
Allah bless him and give him peace, said,

Choose well for your seed [offspring],

marry suitable women and

marry your daughters

to suitable men

(Ibn Majah, 1968)

And he, Allah bless him and give him peace, related that
Allah Mighty and Majestic said,

My love is obligatory

for those who love each other

for My sake

(Ahmad, 1626)

Love in Islam

*T*HE PROPHET, Allah bless him and give him peace, said: "Whoever possesses three qualities tastes through them the sweetness of faith. First, that he should love Allah and His Messenger, Allah bless him and give him peace, above all else; second, that he should love someone solely for the sake of Allah; and third, that he should abhor reverting to disbelief after Allah has rescued him from it, as he would abhor being thrown into the hellfire" (Bukhari, 16).

As someone seeking to draw closer to Allah, your primary objective in marrying is to choose a mate who will help you do this, and thus encourage you to love him or her for His sake. If you are looking for romantic love, then consider the Prophet's, Allah bless him and give him peace, words, "Your love for a thing makes you deaf and blind" (Abu Dawud, 5130). Neither of these qualities is desirable of someone whose aim is to betake himself to Allah. Choosing a spouse should be based on factors that will assist you in the afterlife, not merely the transitory dunya (this world). Then, Allah willing, your love will be both tempered and blessed.

Choosing someone for the sake of Allah means that you should select your mate based upon how seriously he or she is trying to draw closer to Allah, and not simply how physically, intellectually, or even emotionally attractive they may seem. However, you should keep in mind that just because someone is trying to draw closer to Allah Mighty and Majestic, it does not mean they are faultless or even suitable. You need to make all the necessary inquiries.

The purest form of love is to love someone because of Allah's love for that person's iman (faith). Islam calls for lasting love in a marriage of mutual respect, together with the intention of providing your spouse their rights, as a means of drawing nearer to Allah.

In choosing a spouse, there are some points to stress and some notions to discard. We are all, to a certain extent, the product of our environment. Particularly for new Muslims, this means we enter Islam with a variety of preconceptions and outlooks that mediate how we perceive things. Although strongly encouraged by Western culture, marrying solely for romantic love does not usually bring a lasting relationship. Even though it promises to stay forever, there are numerous examples around to prove otherwise. This lustful love can disappear spontaneously; like any other passion, it vanishes as freely as it rises.

The main danger in romantic love is that it tends to result in excessive attachment to the loved one. Consequently, much anxiety occurs when the beloved is absent or aban-dons you, causing your attachment to Allah Almighty and His Messenger, Allah bless him and give him peace, to weaken, if not be lost entirely. If you are captive to this type of romantic love, then consider the words of Sheikh Nif-fari, "Desire is a fire that eats away decency in which alone resides dignity."

Most young adults are in love with love. Falling or being in-love is a pleasant state of excitement, with intense ecstasy at the onset and extreme anguish over the ending. Roman-tic love is a drug that withers away; it always ends. You are conditioned to expect that when you meet the *right* person, fireworks will go off, the world will change in the twinkling of an eye and you will live happily ever after. Though you never see living examples of such happiness, your nafs guar-antees that *you* will be the exception.

While *in love*, one idealizes the beloved and for a while everything is wonderful. When this magic wears off, as it must eventually, you are shocked and hurt to discover that the person you thought was so perfect is really just an ordi-nary person with all the usual flaws. You grieve over the loss of the image that was your source of bliss. This is the kind of trick your nafs uses to fool you into believing *this one thing* is what is really going to make you happy and satisfied.

Many couples today have no idea what to do when they fall out of love. They are even more distraught if they entered the marriage waiting for—but never finding—that romantic love in the first place. Thus, the immature destroy their lives searching for this ephemeral drug of being *in love*.

This is why divorce rates are so high. Did you ever wonder where the expression 'the honeymoon is over' came from? Is it the honeymoon being over or the drug wearing off?

Many, but not all, marriages have a honeymoon stage. The test in life is what you do after the honeymoon stage. It always ends. Is it reasonable or responsible to hasten to a new relationship every year or so—when the honeymoon is over—in order to maintain that ecstasy of being in love?

If the being in love state is over or it never happened in the first place, it does not matter because everyone ends up at the same place of having to develop a healthy loving relationship as it is not the magic of *romantic love* that makes a relationship work. You must cultivate the relationship you will share for the rest of your life. Your beautiful Islamic marriage will happen if you both are mature and committed to a life together, through thick and thin.

Feel assured that in an Islamic marriage, love exists—not necessarily the idealized romantic love—and it grows each year as the result of experiencing each other's beautiful Islamic behavior and manners. Many people are looking for romantic love and are willing to waste or destroy their lives trying to find it.

Love in Islam is nourishing to both the giver and the receiver. Learning to love takes practice and time, especially in an era that focuses so intensely on romantic love. In marriages that thrive, the transitory in-love state is replaced by mutual-loving; loving that is healthy, stable, and balanced.

Common Sense *before* Marriage

*A*LLAH ALMIGHTY CAUTIONS, "Do not marry unbelieving women until they believe... even though she attracts you. Nor marry believing women to unbelievers until they believe... even though he attracts you. Unbelievers do but beckon you to the Fire" (Qur'an, 2: 221).

The Messenger of Allah, Allah bless him and give him peace, advised, "Keeping good company is like sitting with someone who carries musk. Keeping bad company is like sitting with someone who blows on coals. Good company lets you enjoy the pleasant scent even if you yourself do not carry it. Bad company is detrimental in two ways: you will either burn your clothes, or you will smell bad" (Bukhari, 5534).

Who is more likely to affect you than your spouse? For this reason, you need to evaluate a prospective spouse to ensure that you are both in agreement regarding your inclinations and goals. Your potential mate must be someone who is seeking Allah, be willing to do what is necessary to reach Him by following the Sacred Law and share the desire of being with those who will help and encourage you on your journey to Him. Make sure your prospective spouse is committed to applying the Sacred Law, especially when angry or under stress. If you do not make this your criterion, then you will encounter distraction and annoyance in your struggle to Allah rather than help.

The Messenger of Allah, Allah bless him and give him peace, said, "Let each of you have a grateful heart, a tongue that makes dhikr (remembrance), and a believing and virtuous wife to help him prepare for the afterlife" (Ibn Majah, 1856). This advice is equally applicable to women.

'Umar (Allah be well pleased with him) used to say, "After belief in Allah, a man can have no better gift than a virtuous wife. Some women are an irreplaceable prize; others are shackles from which there is no ransom." As many women can attest, this is also true of husbands.

Ask your prospective spouse all the questions you have. Assume nothing. For example, if the man looks religious, do not assume that he does not smoke, prays Fajr on time, is not planning on having four wives, and so forth. And if the woman looks religious, do not assume that she knows how to be a good Muslim wife, prays regularly, and so forth. Ask about all matters that concern you. Ask about all issues concerning marriage, from house to spouse. Do not take anything for granted. Be clear. Do not interpret the answer if it was not explicit—ask again. Correctly understanding the prospective spouse's responses to these issues is of the utmost importance to you. This insight will help you make your decision about whether to marry this person or not.

Finding out about the person prior to marriage is not against Islamic adab (etiquette). Rather, it is best that all relevant matters be brought to light in order for you to make a sound decision.

A sensible choice from the beginning helps to avoid much anguish and many obstacles in the future. People often fail to realize how serious marriage is until after having wed; it is wise to think things through. Be honest with yourself about your own faults and needs; look critically at who you are thinking about marrying and then perform the Prayer of Guidance (Istikhara) several times. The outcome of the prayer does not necessarily appear in a dream; rather, if matters move smoothly and the way is opened, this is considered a positive response to the prayer.

The following is a story about asking Allah Most Wise by way of praying Istikhara and behaving responsibly after acting upon it. It was said that once a righteous man married a pious woman. On his wedding night, he found his bride very unattractive. Upon seeing his aversion to her, she asked him had he not prayed Istikhara about marrying her. He replied in the affirmative. She then asked him if he thought his Lord had deceived him. Upon seeing her wisdom, he consummated the marriage and they conceived a righteous religious son.

Success in following the Istikhara rests on both spouses being pious and behaving in a righteous, God-fearing manner. If each spouse does not adhere to this beautiful Islamic decorum, surely they will have no one but themselves to blame if they lack a felicitous marriage.

Fallacies about Happiness

YOU SHOULD BE HAPPY with a prospective spouse as he or she *is*, rather than anticipating an array of future improvements. After marriage, some changes naturally take place, though they may be different from those you expect or want.

Long-standing personal traits seldom change much, unless a person is fighting them, and even then, it takes time. For example, if you are lazy before marriage, you will most probably remain lazy unless you are actively trying to change. Virtually any habit can be broken if the will exists. However, going into a marriage depending on this transformation is unrealistic, risky and ill-advised.

If something physical bothers you about the other person, then decide before marrying if you can actually live with it. It is wrong to criticize or express aversion to a physical characteristic in your spouse, especially when you clearly knew it before marriage. This type of audacity, hardheartedness, immaturity and selfishness will devastate a

Muslim's life, namely your spouse's. This is haram. For instance, if it really bothers you and you know that you will never be happily married to a fat woman, then you should not marry a chubby girl; after marriage and having children, she will most likely become overweight. Be honest with yourself and then live with your decision. This means that you commit yourself to abide by the choice you have made bearing with all consequences, for better or for worse.

Marriage is one of the greatest trusts two people can take on and the husband and wife should respect it as such. Allah Mighty and Exalted says: "O believers! Betray not Allah and the Messenger, and betray not your trusts" (Qur'an, 8:27).

We live in an age of recycling, deleting, changing the channel, or just turning the whole thing off. For this reason, it is quite difficult to find someone who is committed to and responsible for the consequences of their actions. Being unaccustomed to this accountability makes it weigh heavily upon us. We want out as soon as the instant gratification ceases. Marriage should not be abused in this manner. It takes work to make it work. Surely, you are accountable for all your decisions and behavior. This is why it is vitally important to wisely pick and choose in the first place. Your choice will determine the efforts needed to secure a happy marriage and to lead a life pleasing to Allah, Mighty and Majestic. Not living up to your preconceptions is no excuse to escape and leave behind the responsibilities of a home, children, and the shattered life of a fellow

Muslim. Muslims are expected to be responsible and should behave accordingly.

A relationship of excessive dependency is likewise unhealthy and destructive. No one can single-handedly make another person happy. To burden your partner with the demands and expectations of making you happy never brings success. Rather, it causes many obstacles in the marriage and the state of unhappiness continues, if it does not increase. A person with these types of expectations or needs should find contentment in themselves before getting married.

Another common fallacy is that having a baby necessarily brings stability, security, and happiness. The reality is that during the first couple of years, a baby takes much more than it gives. Having a baby cannot fulfill desperate dreams of contentment. A baby should be brought into a healthy, stable marriage—not be expected to create one. A person with these expectations needs to mature before attempting to have a child.

With a little optimism, much good can happen. Endeavor to improve your attitude and outlook on life in general. (If you do not know how to do this, then find a book that can help.) Realizing that you are responsible for yourself and not expecting others to make you happy is a good start. It is not people that make you happy, rather it is with people your happiness is shared.

True fulfillment comes through your relationship with Allah, Mighty and Majestic. "Surely in the remembrance of Allah do hearts find satisfaction" (Qur'an, 13:28).

One of the best ways to find fulfillment and happiness is through applying the Qur'anic and Prophetic advice, which is to say as much as possible on a daily basis: "Allâhumma salli 'alâ Sayyidinâ Muḥammadin wa 'alâ alihi wa saḥbihi wa sallim" (O Allah, bless our liegelord Muhammad and his folk and Companions and give them peace).

As well as, "Astaghfiru Llâh" (I ask forgiveness of Allah); or you may say: "Astaghfiru Llâha l-'Aẓima lladhî lâ ilâha illâ Huwa l-Ḥayya l-Qayyûma wa atûbu ilayh: (I ask forgiveness of Allah Most Great, who there is no god besides, the Living, the Ever-Subsistent, and I repent to Him).

Additional Factors

OU MUST KEEP IN MIND, however, that while the afore-
mentioned criteria are the most important in choosing
a spouse, additional factors should also be considered.
Among the most important of these is compatibility. When
assessing a potential spouse, although you cannot expect
total harmony, you need to look for someone you can comfortably live and work with on the way to Allah. Ask all the
questions you feel are important to you; do not assume anything. The fact that two people are good Muslims does not
necessarily mean that they will make a good couple. For this
reason, it is essential that you feel comfortable with the person you are about to marry. The distinction is important:
being good is one thing, being compatible is something
else. There is no need to fool or force yourself merely
because someone is practicing Islam or appears to be 'a
good catch'.

In choosing a partner, it is to your utmost advantage to
marry someone who views and lives Islam as you do. This
will minimize the chance of conflict later. The greater your

compatibility and more similar your goals and outlooks, the more likely the prospect of a successful marriage becomes. If you are both religious, do not assume compatibility in your views of Islam and its practice. This is your chance to discuss all matters that are relevant and important to you; do not take anything for granted.

It is recommended that you be somewhat physically attracted to each other. This, however, should not be the main motivating factor. It is easy to be seduced by physical beauty, but is it really what you want to base your future on? Lust often blinds you to the true nature of things. And since marriage is meant to be for life, is it not better to make your decision with discernment rather than irrational lust?

If you are not attracted to the prospective spouse, you must be honest with yourself and seriously consider how important this is to you. It is natural and healthy to want to be reasonably attracted to the person you marry; however, attracted does not mean smitten. There are many tests and trials in life, so where they are avoidable, avoid them.

Help yourself build a life that pleases Allah Mighty and Majestic by marrying a pious, righteous person. In Islam, marriage is a source of tranquility, with the husband and the wife interacting with tenderness conducive to each other's spiritual growth.

Some Muslims might scoff at the idea of such a union, preferring instead to pile trial upon trial, test upon test, and purposely choose a spouse who will be a source of struggle and self-punishment rather than support. For example, a man might, in a fit of zeal, seek out the least attractive woman around, thinking that this will somehow show his nafs (lower self) who is boss. Bliss in the next life does not entail a hellish marriage in this one. Only someone interested in self-punishment would embrace this uncalled for suffering. Islam does not ask this of us. It is reported that the Messenger of Allah, Allah bless him and give him peace, never chose between two matters except that he chose the easier of the two, as long as there was no sin in it (Bukhari, 3560).

The wise way, then, is to intelligently and diplomatically sublimate the nafs, rooting out the characteristics inconsistent with the Sacred Law and replacing them with those blessed by Allah.

The most important consideration is to choose someone who will facilitate a life of love of Allah. And this involves mainly finding a person who takes their Islam (personal submission to the Lord of the worlds) seriously and lives by it.

Men as Men
Women as Women

TODAY, Muslim men and women, especially those influenced by Western ideals, lack an understanding of their gender roles. Among non-Muslims in the west, it is culturally acceptable, if not encouraged, for women to behave like men and men like women. It seems as though women worldwide are struggling to cast off anything that speaks of their womanhood. Men, too, often fail to attain genuine manhood as traditionally understood.

This confusion has historically been foreign to Muslims. But now, the non-Islamic notion that equality lies in a 'unisex' society has overtaken us. Muslims have become influenced by this cultural and emotional corruption. Recognition and affirmation of the Islamic standards of equality and division of roles is essential. The Messenger of Allah, Allah bless him and give him peace, cursed masculine women and feminine men (Bukhari, 5885).

Muslims, male and female, need to cleanse themselves of the cultural pollution that has tainted them. We must return to our fitra (true natures), and accept Allah's definition of equality. This certainly does not entail having the same role in life or manifesting the same outward characteristics.

Allah Mighty and Majestic loves righteousness with no preference to gender:

For men and women who surrender to Allah,

for believing men and women,

for obedient men and women,

for men and women who speak the truth,

for men and women who are patient and constant,

for men and women who are humble,

for men and women who give in charity,

for men and women who fast (and restrain themselves),

for men and women who guard their chastity,

and for men and women who engage much in Allah's praise,

Allah has prepared for them forgiveness and a great reward (Qur'an, 33:35).

For the Muslim, equality is in being given the choice of having taqwa (God-fearingness) and of sublimating the nafs (the lower self). Everyone has been given a nafs as well as the ability and opportunity to let it heed or transgress against Allah's commands. Our task, through sustained effort, is to induce our nafs into a state of submission to Allah Most High and His commands. This is the true measure of a human being's rank over another. All other seeming disparities are transient and of little concern in the path to Allah.

Furthermore, Allah's criterion of equality, or rather, superiority, is not one of gender: "O mankind, We have created you male and female ... that you may know one another. Surely the noblest among you in the sight of Allah is the most God-fearing of you" (Qur'an, 49:13).

Created Different

THE OBVIOUS physiological, biological, and emotional differences created in men and women lead to natural differences in the division of labor. In the family, as in every group, it is necessary that there be an acknowledged leader, someone invested with the final word. Allah has given this function to the man. In spirit and fact, the matter is often established quite amiably. Scholars have said, "Justice [in enforcing rights and prerogatives] is only needed in the absence of love."

In a marriage based on love, compassion and journeying to Allah, a dictatorial atmosphere will not develop. Decisions will be made by honest discussion and deference to the wishes of your spouse. "Verily Allah loves those who act aright" (Qur'an, 3:76). However, when dissent arises and a resolution needs to be reached, the burden of that responsibility falls upon the man, who should perform the Prayer of Guidance (Istikhara) and its outcome should be followed.

Otherwise, the scholars say that the wife is the queen of her home and in her 'palace' the husband should let her do what she wants. If she asks him to do something permissible and possible, like picking up his clothes, he should comply.

'A'isha (Allah be well pleased with her) was asked what the Messenger of Allah, Allah bless him and give him peace, did at home. She answered that he was at the service of his family, meaning that he assisted his family in their chores, and if the time for prayer came, he would go out to pray (Bukhari, 676). In another hadith, she replied that he did as any man does; he cleaned his shoes and picked up his clothes (Ahmad, 24228).

You can see that the Prophetic example is one of cooperation and harmony, not arrogance and discourtesy. "If you love Allah, follow me [the Messenger of Allah]: Allah will love you and forgive you your sins; for Allah is Oft-Forgiving, Most Merciful" (Qur'an, 3:31).

The Prophet, Allah bless him and give him peace, stated, "Every one of you is a guardian (of his immediate charge) and is responsible for them... The man is a guardian over his family and responsible for them. The woman is a guardian over her husband's house and responsible for it..." (Bukhari, 893). Based on this, Islam distributes the tasks between wife and husband, and both are responsible for creating a happy Islamic environment in the home. Allah Mighty and Majestic says, "O you who believe, protect yourself and your family from the fire" (Qur'an, 66:6).

The wife is given the home as her domain. In maintaining the home, she should keep it clean, tidy, welcoming and peaceful, thus protecting it against the intrusion of devils and jinns. The husband is responsible for supporting and maintaining his family. This was how the Messenger of Allah, Allah bless him and give him peace, divided the work between his daughter Fatima (Allah be well pleased with her) and her husband 'Ali (may Allah ennoble his countenance).

Men and women marry in order to complement each other's nature. A man marries a woman for her loving kindness and tenderness, not for a masculine disposition. Likewise, a woman marries a man to share her life with someone who is mature and dependable, not to be dominated by a tyrant or left to fend for herself. Many Westerners have difficulty in understanding these and other differences in gender roles in Islam. The majority have been raised in a self-centered way. Everyone is 'their own person' on an 'equal footing', not a team player. In other words, everyone is 'free' from any responsibility and 'free' to do whatever they want.

In the 'me-myself-and-I' society of immediate gratification and instant everything, *patience, endurance and commitment* are very unusual if not unheard of all together. These noble characteristics are an affront to the contemporary cultures where continuity has little or no value. This leads to a constant demand for rights with little or no consideration for responsibilities or duties. This is detrimental to marriage and often leads to resentment and frustration when either spouse feels that their needs are not being met. Though allowing for personal flexibility, Islam promotes a separation of gender roles as a means to attaining the fullest potential as an individual and a partner in marriage. Mutual respect and kindness are primary elements towards forming a good marriage. A good marriage is the result of substantial work, not chance. Your input is either positive or negative, and you live with the results.

Many Muslims, old and new, must overcome both their own selfishness and typically western attitudes. They need to understand and accept their fitra (natural disposition) and be satisfied with the blessings that Allah has given each gender, male or female. It is the corruption and desertion of our fitra that makes it difficult to develop a Muslim character. However, you can develop that noble and beautiful Muslim character with sincere and sustained effort. It is not easy to become one of the beloveds of Allah Mighty and Majestic, but you should strive, since it is possible and others have succeeded.

It is natural for newcomers to Islam to look for a guide or role model, which is occasionally provided by an ethnic Muslim. Whether such guidance proves positive or negative depends on whether, and how much, the role model adheres to the Sacred Law. You should follow what is Islamic of their behavior, and discard what is not. The Sacred Law according to the four schools of jurisprudence is the yardstick pious Muslims use to measure everyone and everything.

Criterion for Selection

THE MAJOR CONSIDERATION in choosing a spouse is finding someone who views life and religion the same as you. It does not matter if religion plays a major or minor role in your life—as long as you have a complimentary view. Even more essential than sharing the same views about life and religion is the actual application of your views. It is one thing to agree in theory, but it is very difficult if the assumed application of the common views is different. Actual application must be extremely similar if not identical. For example, in theory you both believe the hijab is obligatory but when it comes to application one says, "I believe the hijab is obligatory, but I do not want you to wear it in the West." Or you both assume that the other prays all the prayers on time and would not accept otherwise, but when asked, the person says, "I believe one should pray the five prayers but because of my work schedule, I do not always do them." Again, make sure the theory and application is compatible, if not identical, to yours.

The other real consideration is the circumstances the prospective spouse lives in, as well as those they were raised in. Today, many families are dysfunctional in various ways. Consider the potential issues this background might entail. Investigate those concerns. Then thoroughly discuss the relevant items that concern you in order to make a wise choice.

Save yourself a big heartache...if you marry a man who is committed to spending the rest of his life living with his family, do not expect to gain much when you try asserting your Sacred Law right to your own accommodations six months later. Or, if you want to live an isolated life with a closed, private, nuclear family—do not marry a woman from a large, tight-knit extended family, and then expect her to carry on and be happy when you try to detach her from them.

Be realistic and honest with yourself about the person and/or situation you are considering. Do not go into a marriage hoping the person or situation will miraculously change. That almost never happens. Do not believe your nafs when it says, "This is the exception."

Rather, marry the person who is acceptable to you from the start. You will still find marriage to that person satisfactory if the reforms you had designed do not occur.

Or, marry into a situation that is reasonable to you from the start. If it does not develop as you might have imagined, then it will not cause you resentment.

It is crucial that you ask yourself before marriage, "If my future spouse or situation does not change to what I desire or require, can I live with that?" This is the time that you must be painstakingly honest with yourself, otherwise you will find yourself after everyone has gone alone with the spouse and/or situation you have chosen. Asking this question after marriage really does not do you much good. By then, if you are asking this question, then you already know that you have made a big mistake. It is better to be honest with yourself now, rather than be trapped and unhappy later. (See above: Fallacies about Happiness)

What to Look for in a Man

ASIDE FROM THOSE QUALITIES that differ from person to person and are particular to each potential couple, one should look for specific virtues. In a husband these are:

- Piety
- A halal (lawful) income, sufficient to support his household
- Basic Islamic knowledge, because Allah says: "Protect yourself and your family from the fire" (Qur'an, 66:6).
- Contentment
- Ability to make mature judgments
- Ability to understand and think soundly
- A forgiving nature, tolerance, and an even temper
- Patience
- Generosity
- Responsibility, protectiveness, and cooperation
- Being from a decent, stable family. The Prophet, Allah bless him and give him peace, said: "Choose well for

your seed, marry suitable women and marry your daughters to suitable men" (Ibn Majah, 1968).

- Good appearance and bodily cleanliness. (The intended bride may look at the man who wishes to marry her as many times as she needs to make her decision.)

What to Look for in a Woman

*T*HERE ARE IMPORTANT qualities and virtues to look for in a wife and mother for your children. They are:

- Piety. The Prophet, Allah bless him and give him peace, said: "A woman is married for her wealth, her lineage, her beauty or her religion. Choose the religious one or you will lose" (Bukhari, 5090).

- Affectionate and easygoing nature. The Prophet, Allah bless him and give him peace, said: "Marry loving, fertile women" (Nasa'i, 3227).

- Ability to make mature judgments

- Ability to understand and think soundly

- Obedience

- Patience

- Contentment. The Messenger of Allah, Allah bless him and give him peace, said: "I was shown hell and the majority of its inhabitants were ungrateful women." The Companions asked, "Were they ungrateful to Allah?" "No," he replied, "[it was because] of their ingratitude to their husbands and denying the goodness done to them.

Even if you were generous to her for a lifetime, as soon as she experiences anything she dislikes from you [her husband], she tells you that she has never seen any goodness from you" (Muslim, 907).

- Being from a decent, stable family. The Prophet, Allah bless him and give him peace, said: "Choose well for your seed, marry suitable women and marry your daughters to suitable men" (Ibn Majah, 1968). As well as: "Beware of a beautiful girl of bad background" (Musnad al-Shihab, 957).

- Good appearance and bodily cleanliness. (When seeking marriage, a man may see only the face and hands of the intended bride. The Messenger of Allah, Allah bless him and give him peace, said after a girl reaches puberty it is not permissible to see other than her face and hands (Abu Dawud, 4104)).

'Ali (may Allah ennoble his countenance) used to say: "Three vices in a man are virtues in a woman: stinginess, vanity and timidity. If she is stingy, she will watch her own property and that of her husband. If she is vain, she will not condescend to engage in dubious conversation with anybody. If she is timid, she will be cautious of everything; she will not venture out of her house needlessly, and will avoid disputable places for fear of displeasing her husband."

Lastly, a man is responsible for choosing a righteous mother for his children. The Messenger of Allah, Allah bless him and give him peace, advised: "Select the best place for your seed, the righteous wife" (Daraqutni). When making this decision he should make sure that the lady of his choice understands and is eager to enter her jihad (struggle) with a spirit of taqwa (God-fearingness) and cooperation. In other words, he should choose someone aspiring to be a righteous wife and mother. Likewise, the woman should choose someone who is earnest about being a righteous husband and father. You are going to be held responsible in this world and the next for the choice you make—so you need not rush.

What to Avoid

*Y*OUR SPOUSE'S GOOD CHARACTER is an important element for peace of mind and help in your religion. Make note of those specific traits and manners that you find unsuitable in a spouse. With these well in mind, you should also avoid the one who is:

- irreligious or immoral
- ill-tempered or the short-tempered
- arrogant or conceited
- unsatisfied
- miserly
- a tyrant in word and deed, or the one who lacks understanding and compassion
- immature, weak-minded, or the one who constantly asks for or threatens divorce
- impatient
- irresponsible
- loafer, grumbler, or complainer
- hypochondriac and malingerer

- habitually criticizes and belittles

- constantly reminds you of favors they have done

- pines for a former beloved, a child from a previous marriage, parents, or others

- covets everything they see and pressures you to buy it

- talks too much

3

Rights and Obligations

When faith is sincere, behavior is righteous

$\mathcal{F}$IRST AND FOREMOST, we are all servants of Allah. All we do should be done in this light. In order to do this, however, we must become acquainted with what Allah says. Here are some of His words for thought as well as application:

- "Fear the Day when you shall be brought back to Allah. Then shall every soul be paid what it earned" (Qur'an, 2:281).

- "It is not fitting for a believer, man or woman, when a matter has been decided by Allah and His Messenger, to have any opinion about their decision. Whosoever disobeys Allah and His Messenger has gone astray into manifest error" (Qur'an, 33:36).

- "Allah commands justice, the doing of good, and charity to kith and kin, and He forbids all shameful deeds, and injustice and rebellion: He instructs you that you may receive admonition. Fulfill the covenant of Allah when you have entered into it, and break not your oaths after you have confirmed them: Indeed you have made Allah your surety; for Allah knows all that you do" (Qur'an, 16:90-1).

- "Short is the enjoyment of this world; and the Hereafter is better for those who fear Allah" (Qur'an, 4:77).

- "As to those who believed and did righteous deeds, their Lord will admit them to His mercy; that will be the achievement for all to see" (Qur'an, 45:30).

- "Allah loves those who do good" (Qur'an, 3:148).

- "He who obeys the Messenger, obeys Allah: But if any turn away, We have not sent you to watch over their (evil deeds)" (Qur'an, 4:80).

Clearly here Allah commands that we follow His Messenger, Allah bless him and give him peace. The following are among his sayings, Allah bless him and give him peace, that are considered pivotal to the religion. "Verily Allah the Almighty has laid down religious duties, so do not neglect them; He has set boundaries, so do not overstep them; He has prohibited some things, so do not violate them; about some things He was silent—out of compassion for you, not forgetfulness—so seek not after them" (Daraqutni).

As well as: "Do you know who is impoverished?" The Companions replied that the impoverished is the one who has no money or property. He, Allah bless him and give him peace, refuted this and said: "The impoverished of my followers is one who will come on the Day of Judgment with a good record of prayers and fasting and zakat, but he has abused somebody; slandered someone; taken the goods of another; has killed someone or beaten yet another. Then all the wronged persons will receive a part of the aggressors' good deeds. Should his good deeds fall short of recompensing his aggression, then those who have been wronged will

have their sins and faults transferred from them to him,
and he will be thrown into the Hellfire" (Muslim, 2581).

And, "Verily your Lord has a right over you, your self
has a right over you, your family has a right over you, thus
give everyone who has a right their right" (Bukhari, 1968).

Letter and Spirit

THE LETTER: "O YOU WHO BELIEVE! Obey Allah, and obey the Messenger, and those charged with authority among you. If you differ in anything among yourselves, refer it to Allah and His Messenger, if you do believe in Allah and the Last Day: that is best, and most suitable for final determination" (Qur'an, 4:59). "O you who believe, do not be forward in the presence of Allah and His Messenger (but follow behind: do not precede them but be subordinate to them. Do not decide your matters yourselves by your own initiative, but look for the guidance given in Allah's Book and the Way of Life of His Prophet concerning theses matters); and keep you duty to Allah. Allah is Hearer, Knower" (Qur'an, 49:1).

The spirit: "To Allah we belong, and to Him is our return" (Qur'an, 2:156). "O Messenger of Allah tell me something about Islam which I can ask no one but you." He, Allah bless him and give him peace, said: "Say: I believe in Allah—and thereafter be upright" (Muslim, 38). "Verily those who say, 'Our Lord is Allah,' and remain firm (in belief, words and actions), on them shall be no fear, nor shall they grieve" (Qur'an, 46:13).

It is important, especially in marriage, to live a balanced life of the law and spirit; for lacking in either will lead to problems in this world and the next. Many new Muslims mistakenly read books of fiqh (Islamic jurisprudence) as guide books to better living. A cursory look at the rules established by the Sacred Law will often reveal the letter of the law and not necessarily the spirit. Thus, you should keep in mind when reading legal opinions that they often express the minimum of a ruling, or the legal requirement. This should not be understood as providing the exemplary standard for Muslims to live by. That is to say, they tell you what rights you have in front of a judge, not how you should live ideally.

According to the Sacred Law, marriage is a contract of mutual consent. It consists of two simple sentences. A woman or her guardian says, "I marry myself (or my charge) to you." And the man responds immediately, "I accept." These few words have a great legal and spiritual significance. They mean that both husband and wife have freely committed themselves to their marriage and to all its responsibilities.

In spiritual terms, marriage is described as a 'solemn covenant' (Qur'an, 4:21). This covenant is to live in equity and kindness as Allah Almighty has ordered. Consequently, if one does not fulfill this promise in technical terms the contract remains valid; however, one has transgressed the bounds set by Allah and will meet their Lord with this grave sin.

"But when He gave to them of His generosity, they hoarded it and turned away in aversion. So He punished them by putting hypocrisy into their hearts until the day they meet Him, because they broke their promise to Allah and lied" (Qur'an, 9:76-77).

In upholding an Islamic marriage, you do not merely demand and fulfill a series of mutual rights and obligations. Rather, the relationship should be elevated by maintaining a merciful and loving nature, in accordance with that of our beloved Prophet, Allah bless him and give him peace. Allah Most High says: "It is part of the mercy of Allah that you [Muhammad] deal gently with them. Were you severe or harsh-hearted, they would have scattered from about you. So pardon them, and pray forgiveness for them ... put your trust in Allah. Surely Allah loves those who put their trust (in Him)" (Qur'an, 3:159). One should try to be of 'those who are with the Prophet', Allah bless him and give him peace, in spirit: "Muhammad is the Messenger of Allah; and those who are with him are... compassionate amongst each other" (Qur'an, 48:29).

You should make it a policy throughout your life to be grateful for everything Allah gives you. If you do this, you will succeed in your jihad (personal struggle). This includes being grateful for any of your spouse's good qualities so that Allah might improve the rest. "If you thank Allah, verily He will give you more" (Qur'an, 14:7).

Rights or duties are not instruments of abuse for a husband or wife to use against each other. Such conduct indicates a lack of understanding of the spirit of an Islamic marriage and Islam itself. When faith is sincere, behavior is righteous. Allah Almighty says, "Verily the reward of the Hereafter is the best, for those who believe, and are constant in righteousness" (Qur'an, 12:57).

To find detailed information about Islamic marriage contracts please see *Your Islamic Marriage Contract*.

Duties of the Husband

*Y*OU OFTEN FIND literature discussing the duties of the Muslim wife with no mention of those of the husband's. While the wife's role in setting the tone of an Islamic marriage cannot be overstated, the husband also plays a crucial role in determining whether or not the marriage will please Allah.

The most important responsibility of the Muslim husband is to support and maintain his family with a completely halal (lawful) income. The gravity of this cannot be overstressed. Food purchased through non-halal money or means becomes itself haram (unlawful). It is said that if you eat halal, you will do halal; and if you eat haram, you will do haram in spite of yourself. The wives and daughters of the Companions used to tell their husbands and fathers that they could endure hunger but not hell, referring to the consumption of haram food and income. The Messenger of Allah, Allah bless him and give him peace, said, "Surely a body fed on haram will not enter paradise—verily hell is more deserving of that body" (Ahmad, 14032).

A man intending to marry should seriously consider his means of income to ensure that the Sacred Law sanctions it. Matters such as interest, insurance, credit, and in general, any doubtful financial ventures should be avoided as completely as possible. You are much better off living a modest, yet absolutely halal lifestyle than living a luxurious life now and paying dearly later. Whenever in doubt, ask a trustworthy scholar.

A man should not only support and maintain his home and family, but should do so with generosity and pleasure, knowing that this pleases Allah and he will be rewarded accordingly.

It is not unusual for the husband's nafs to enjoy helping strangers and outsiders, while finding it very difficult to fulfill his wife's requests or help at home. From this reaction of his nafs, he should realize that aiding his wife or helping at home should take priority over assisting outsiders. "Spend of what We have provided you before death should come to any of you and he says, 'O my Lord, if only You would defer me unto a near term, so that I may make freewill offering, and so I may become one of the righteous'. But Allah will never defer any soul when its term comes. And Allah is aware of the things you do" (Qur'an, 63:10). It is improper to do this duty to Allah and to your wife resentfully, out of compulsion or habit. A grudging compliance may offer safety from punishment, but will not earn the reward that Allah might otherwise bestow. The Messenger of Allah, Allah bless him and give him peace, assured Muslim men, "You do not spend any sum for the sake of Allah without being rewarded, even if what you spent was for the food you put in the mouth of your wife" (Bukhari, 5354). The weightiness and reality of this responsibility is usually realized only after getting married and then many men feel overwhelmed by it. Thus, it is wise to realistically think through all these aspects before this happens.

A man should know the regulations concerning marriage, divorce and women's issues before marriage, so he can observe the restraints necessary for a halal relationship; such as that a three-fold pronouncement of divorce whether made on three different occasions or one and the same occasion constitutes a final termination of a marriage, rulings on menstruation, and so forth. He must also ensure that his wife knows the 'aqida (tenets of faith), as well as aspects of the Sacred Law that are obligatory for her to know, particularly women-specific regulations such as those governing menstruation, childbirth and motherhood.

A husband should behave well toward his wife, showing patience and tolerance of any shortcomings. Allah Most High says: "Say to My servants, that they say those things that are kindlier. For surely Satan sows dissension among them: for Satan is to man an avowed enemy" (Qur'an, 17:53).

Words or jokes that break a Muslim's heart are not permissible. The constant endeavors of Shaytan and his helpers of trying to create discord between a Muslim couple by every means possible should never be underestimated. Consequently, a righteous husband should not joke crassly or harshly with his wife. With some husbands it is common to joke about taking another wife; this produces insecurity and anger perhaps, but no laughs. And this in turn raises barriers between them. If a husband is looking to have a harmonious relationship with his wife, then he understands how detrimental barriers are and tries to avoid them. The righteous husband exemplifies the Prophetic standard of being lenient, gentle and understanding with his wife: "He [The Messenger of Allah] is gentle to the believers, compassionate" (Qur'an, 9:128).

Managing the home and taking care of the family is exhausting. In order for the wife to fulfill her duties properly there must be support, understanding, tolerance and cooperation. As a scholar stated, a good husband must fulfill a variety of roles: he must be like a father, mother, and sibling to his wife. She left her father, mother, brothers and sisters for him, so she should find in him the gentleness of a father, the compassion of a mother, the leniency of a brother and the companionship of a sister.

It is his duty to make sure she follows Allah's limits: "There is no blame (on women if they appear) before their fathers or their sons, their brothers, or their brothers' sons, or their sisters' sons, or their women... And fear Allah; surely Allah is Witness to all things" (Qur'an, 33:55). This verse means that it is permissible for a woman to unveil only before those mentioned. Thus, according to Islamic rules of gender conduct, he must insist, and if he does not, then she must insist to cover herself in front of his brothers, uncles, his or her male cousins, his sisters' husbands and her sisters' or aunts' husbands; he should not allow free mixing with them.

The Messenger of Allah, Allah bless him and give him peace, said, "Your male-in-laws are like death" (Bukhari, 5232). The meaning of the hadith is that the wife may, if appropriate, mix with her husband's father, grandfather or his sons, grandsons, and that her mixing with any other of his male relatives brings about disaster as terrible as death. The ties created by marriage allow the male relations with easy access to the house, coming and going without suspicion. This opens the door for catastrophe.

In adhering to these duties of righteousness, a believer will aid himself to be well separated from evil on the Day of Judgment. Allah Most High says: "On the Day when every soul will be confronted with all the good it has done and all the evil it has done, it will wish there were a great distance between it and its evil. Allah Himself cautions you. And Allah is full of kindness to those that serve Him" (Qur'an, 3:30). To establish goodness and to serve Allah, the husband should know his wife's rights, how to treat her, his part in her spiritual life, and his responsibility regarding their children.

The Wife's Rights

THE MUSLIM HUSBAND is obliged to provide the following in the fine Islamic manner that draws him near to his Lord, Allah Most Glorious:

- The wife's full mahr (marriage payment), and her daily maintenance of clothing, food and shelter.

- Warm intimacy and companionship, with pleasant and righteous behavior.

- Sexual satisfaction. The husband should maintain the amount that will keep his wife chaste. The Hanafi and Shafi'i scholars generally hold her right to be every four days, however this depends on the wife's need.

- Teaching or providing a means for her to learn her 'personally obligatory religious knowledge' ('ilm al-hal).

Although the list appears short, proper Islamic adherence to it is difficult. As with any type of worship, perfection demands striving and constancy is difficult to maintain.

When scholars are asked: "To whom should one marry one's daughter?" They counsel: "To someone who fears Allah. If he loves her he will be generous with her, and if he dislikes her he will not violate her rights."

Beautiful words to the wise...Be careful if you make a woman cry because Allah Most High counts her tears. A woman came out of the rib of man, not his feet to be walked on, nor his head to be superior over; she came from his side to be his companion, under his arm to be protected, and next to the heart to be loved.

How to Treat Your Wife

" *N*OR SHOULD YOU treat them [women] with harshness... on the contrary live with them on a footing of kindness and equity. If you take a dislike to them it may be that you dislike a thing, and Allah brings about through it a great deal of good" (Qur'an, 4:19).

What more needs to be said when Allah Almighty commands that you live in kindness and equity with your wife? If the husband disobeys Allah's command, what can he expect? Abu Sulaiman al-Darani, when asked about marriage, replied, "It is easier to have patience with a woman than to be in Hell."

The Messenger of Allah, Allah bless him and give him peace, said: "Fear Allah in regard to women. You were given them as a trust from Allah and by the word of Allah, they have become lawful for you" (Muslim, 1218). This clearly states that a wife is a trust, not chattel, in her husband's keeping. And the righteous husband will deal with her accordingly. Before demanding your rights you should be performing your duties.

A man is obliged to protect his wife, treat her with consideration and live harmoniously with her. The good character of a husband not only consists of him not harming his wife, but also in putting up with her shortcomings. Having chosen a righteous woman in the first place, he should find this duty all the easier. And if he does not, he will meet Allah with this enormous sin and possibly lose his wife for not having done so. He should acknowledge the preciousness of his wife, for she is among the greatest of Allah's blessings to him. The Messenger of Allah, Allah bless him and give him peace, stated: "He whom Allah has blessed with a righteous wife has been helped by Allah in half his religion, thus he should fear Allah in the other half" (Tabarani al-Awsat, 976). As well as: "There is nothing more beneficial to a believer after God-fearingness than a righteous wife" (Ibn Majah, 1857).

It is not the husband's right to try to control his wife's mind or ideas. A woman has the right to express her own opinion or criticisms as seen in the Holy Qur'an in surat al-Mujadilah, where Khawla bint Tha'labah complained to the Prophet, Allah bless him and give him peace, and then argued with him about her husband. Women, whether wives or daughters, are under no obligation to consider their husband or father the one and only reference in religious matters. Rather, if a woman has doubt, she is obliged to seek the truth.

In the words of Allah Most High you will find that love, kindness and consideration are reciprocal between spouses, "Women have rights similar to the rights upon them, according to what is equitable. But men have a degree over them; Allah is All-mighty, All-wise" (Qur'an, 2:228). This 'degree' refers to maintenance and financial responsibility, and according to Imam al-Sha'rani, "If the man does not work and support his wife then he loses that degree."

Allah Most High does not permit a man to deal with his wife in a demeaning manner. If he orders her around in a degrading manner she is not obliged to obey him and his degrading her is haram (unlawful). The Prophet, Allah bless him and give him peace, said, "God-fearingness is here (pointing to his heart). It is sufficiently wicked for someone to belittle his fellow Muslim" (Muslim, 2564).

As well as, "A man says something Allah detests that he does not think twice about, for which he plunges into hell" (al-Mustadrak, 137).

The Messenger of Allah, Allah bless him and give him peace, gave this admonition: "Let no male Muslim entertain any malice against a female Muslim. He may dislike one habit in her, but may find another in her which is pleasing" (Muslim, 1469).

Allah Mighty and Majestic has decreed: "Verily, I have forbidden oppression for Myself and I have made it forbidden amongst you. Thus do not oppress one another" (Muslim, 2577). Remember your wife is Allah's servant and not yours.

"O you who believe, stand out firmly for Allah, as witnesses to fair dealing, and let not hatred towards any person induce you to act unjustly against him. Be just: that is next to piety. And fear Allah, for Allah is well acquainted with all that you do. To those who believe and do deeds of righteousness has Allah promised forgiveness and a great reward" (Qur'an, 5:8-9).

Sheikhs say that spiritually accomplished men do not react in a nasty way. They deal with people, especially their wife and children, and problems such that everyone and everything benefits from their gentleness and awareness of Allah, Mighty and Majestic. They listen and respond with mercy because of the God-fearingness in their heart.

Disciplining a wife is an often-misunderstood topic. Contrary to the beliefs of some, physical abuse is haram. A woman is not obliged to tolerate it at all, for any amount of time. The details of disciplining a wife as well as the definition of 'physical abuse' must be taken from a reliable book of Sacred Law.

It is incumbent upon both husband and wife to know, and seek to live by the Islamic jurisprudence (fiqh) of marriage. Following one of the four schools of Sacred Law provides this knowledge. By knowing and living the commands of Allah, one can hope for real tawfiq (success granted by Allah) in life as well as in marriage.

The spirit of Allah's commands can be grasped by reading the Qur'an and hadiths; however, the letter of Allah's commands are known through the traditional scholars of Sacred Law who are qualified to deduce the legal rulings from the Qur'an and hadiths. Believing that you can deduce legal rulings from the Qur'an and hadiths without being properly trained in the Islamic sciences is a hazardous mistake—for we live in a perilous age of arrogance coupled with ignorance.

Helping Your Wife's Spiritual Life

"THE BELIEVERS, MEN AND WOMEN, are protectors, one of another: they enjoin what is just and forbid what is evil: They observe regular prayers, practice regular charity, and obey Allah and His Messenger. On them will Allah pour His mercy: for Allah is Exalted in power, Wise" (Qur'an, 9:71).

The husband should provide the means for his wife to learn, apply her knowledge and grow in her faith and nearness to Allah Mighty and Majestic. If he chooses a person who thinks that he shares her spiritual ambition, then she will be rightly disappointed and angry if he frustrates that ambition by exhausting her with his worldly demands. Women have devotional obligations to fulfill and need the time and energy for them. Allah Most High says: "Surely man is in the way of loss, except those who believe, and do righteous deeds, and counsel each other unto the truth, and counsel each other to be steadfast" (Qur'an, 103: 2-3).

Some husbands believe that all a woman need know is how to cook, clean and have children. However, can a wife do this properly while ignorant of the religion? It is through knowing and understanding the religion that she can make each of these responsibilities acts of worship, spiritually uplifting for herself and therefore her family. If she does not know the religion, how can she teach her children the love and practice of it? With a spiritually healthy wife, you will get a pleasant and loving homemaker. This way everyone wins.

If a husband really believes that supporting his wife's spiritual needs is irrelevant, then he has only himself to blame for the lack of any manifestation of Islam, or baraka (blessings) in his wife, in his children and in his house, which can no longer be called a home.

Allah Mighty and Majestic says: "Protect yourself [husband/father] and your family from the fire" (Qur'an, 66:6).

The Husband's Responsibility Regarding Children

PRIOR TO MARRIAGE, the would-be husband is responsible for selecting a righteous mother for his children.

The husband is financially obligated to support his children. They are a trust from Allah for which he will be accountable on the Day of Judgment. It is essential that a father ensure his children are fed from lawful sources.

He should teach them to respect and honor their mother. He is also responsible for inculcating good manners and discipline in them. They should be taught modesty, contentment and proper etiquette regarding food, drink and dress. He should teach them not to talk excessively, to never swear or lie and to be truthful and honest.

He should teach them their religion in stages. He should instruct them in everything regarding Sacred Law that is obligatory for the individual to know until these become engraved in their hearts. He should warn them against things that are not acceptable in Islam until they themselves fear committing such violations.

The husband is obliged to protect his children from bad company—which is the primary source of all evil. Abu

Hurayra related that the Messenger of Allah, Allah bless him and give him peace, said: "A person is upon the faith of his friend, so take care who you make friends with" (Tirmidhi, 2378). This applies to all Muslims, young and old. Naturally, duties concerning children apply equally to boys and girls.

Parents must 'do' Islam as well as 'speak' it. Actions speak louder and teach better than words. Children observe the actions as well as the hypocrisy of their parents. If actions are contrary to Islamic behavior, this is very confusing to the child. This will cause a loss of respect or disregard for religious obligations and regulations.

Children are very impressed by and have admiration for their father. If the father is active in his children's lives in a loving and caring way, then he will be the most important man in their life. If he is unavailable or detached from their daily lives, this will force them to look for a substitute. Children have a strong natural need for a 'father' figure in their life. Sons have a special need to be approved of by their father—if they do not get this approval, they often suffer from a lack of confidence or self-acceptance well into their own manhood.

The Wife's Obligations

*T*HE WIFE MUST FULFILL the following rights of her husband in the lively and lovely way that pleases Allah Mighty and Majestic:

- Raise their children in an Islamic manner. This requires great care and general knowledge, as well as time, patience, and wisdom, especially in this age of confusion and negative external influences.

- Obey him in his request for sexual intimacy (see Desire, below).

- Protect herself, his house, his wealth, and his children in his absence.

In the Hanafi school, if the man has a high sex drive and the wife does not, then she should comply to the degree that she is capable, thereby fulfilling the duty Allah has asked of her. Some scholars regard 'capability' as meaning physical readiness, allowing for her need to be able to manage her other duties: raising her children, cleaning, cooking, washing, and learning the obligatory knowledge of her religion. Obviously, illness is a cause of incapability in this matter. If the husband finds this unbearable, he should seek pertinent advice about how to deal with this problem.

Despite divine encouragement for moderation, a man's right remains. In the Maliki school, for example, a man may make love with his wife eight times a day or four times during the day and four times during the night. It should be noted that a wife rarely refuses her husband if she is actually receiving her own rights (see Sunnas of Intimate Contact, below).

Women should never make sexual intimacy a game of denial or manipulation. In Islam, there are no reservations about halal (permissible) sexual intercourse. It is not the 'original sin', nor is it something dirty or disgusting. Had it been so, the Messenger of Allah, Allah bless him and give him peace, would have abstained from it.

On the contrary the Prophet, Allah bless him and give him peace, in a long hadith said: "... in the sexual act of each of you there is a charity." The Companions asked: "O Messenger of Allah, when one of us fulfils his sexual desire will he have some reward for that?" He, Allah bless him and give him peace, said: "Do you not think that were he to act upon it unlawfully he would be sinning? Likewise, if he has acted upon it lawfully he will have a reward" (Muslim, 1006). Allah Most High has made it lawful in marriage and a natural aspect of our human biology.

The Messenger of Allah, Allah bless him and give him peace, said: "There is not a man who calls his wife and she refuses him without Allah being angry with her until her husband is pleased with her" (Muslim, 1736).

And, "If a man call his wife to his bed and she refuses and he goes to sleep angry with her, the angels curse her until morning" (Bukhari, 2998).

These hadiths speak of the sacredness of this responsibility the wife has towards her husband, and the need for her to take it seriously. They all testify to the gravity of this matter and that denial must not be made into a game—the consequences are too serious.

These hadiths must be understood in the context of living your life from beginning to end in accordance with the principles of Islam. For example, if the wife is ill, she is not obliged to comply with her husband's request for sexual intimacy. Rather he should show her the consideration he himself would like to receive.

Nonetheless, the consequences of making denial a game cannot be overstated. In normal circumstances, a pious wife should overcome her nafs, fearing that she might fall into the displeasure and anger of Allah if she avoids her husband.

Allah Mighty and Majestic says: "On no soul does Allah place a burden greater than it can bear. It gets every good that it earns, and it suffers every ill that it earns: (Qur'an, 2:286).

If she is angry or displeased with her husband, she should seize her nafs and seek Allah's pleasure by being kind and loving to him. If she finds this absolutely unbear-able or impossible, perhaps this is not the marriage for her. Thus, she should hasten to find a solution. It is unhealthy and unwise to let these types of problems drag on.

The wife is the center of her home and family. She should be occupied in it, striving to create a loving and pleasant environment. She should be concerned with her own business: taking care of her home and diligently doing her various personal and private 'ibadat (worship) and dhikr (remembrance) of Allah. She should be content with the means Allah Most High gives her husband.

She should not visit or talk with neighbors excessively or needlessly as it interferes with her daily duties. If she goes out with her husband's permission, she must go out in proper hijab (covering) without make-up or perfume. She should not raise her voice or speak with men in the street unnecessarily, even if they are her husband's friends. She should give priority to her husband's rights over her own and those of relatives, without doing so grudgingly, and her munificence will increase the loving tenderness between them.

The wife strives to observe the rights of her husband in his presence and absence, and to make him happy in every-thing she does. Like all acts, these duties should be done for Allah. You must take care not to remind your spouse about all you have done or sacrificed for his sake. This applies equally to men, for it is part of the excellence of a believer. Allah Most High says: "Those who spend their substance in the cause of Allah, and follow not up their gifts with reminders of their generosity or with annoyance, for them their reward is with their Lord. On them shall be no fear, nor shall they grieve" (Qur'an, 2:262).

In addition to generating and preserving a loving atmosphere, the woman is also responsible for keeping her home clean. She must keep the house tidy and free from filth and the ritually unclean, for such things have a profound effect on the spiritual state of the family.

The Messenger of Allah, Allah bless him and give him peace, said: "Verily Allah is clean and He loves cleanliness" (Tirmidhi, 2799).

The devils and jinn like dirty dishes and untidy places. The home of a Muslim is no place for these unwelcome guests, so it is essential that the wife maintain the purity of her family's home. She should ask herself: Is my home in a fit state for the prophets or the awliya' (friends of Allah) to enter? If not, why not? A Muslim should have adab (good manners) at all times, and with everything, for he knows that Allah sees him. The proper adab concerning your home is to keep it clean.

Many women, raised in cultures that view the idea that 'a woman's place is in the home' as sexist and backwards, may be repelled by the fact that their home and family are indeed their main responsibility. They should attempt to adjust their cultural mores, and reflect on the immeasurable social chaos that has been caused in the West by the woman abandoning the home.

The wife should be attentive to her children, and keep their secrets. She should not insult them nor imprecate against them as some do by saying things like: "May Allah take you," or "May Allah give you a headache like the one you have caused me." The Messenger of Allah, Allah bless him and give him peace, said, "Do not make a prayer upon yourselves except for that which is good, verily the angels say 'Ameen' to what you say" (Muslim, 920).

When doing your duty becomes tiresome, you need to remind yourself that it is done for Allah. Allah Most Exalted says: "Whoever submits his whole self to Allah and is a doer of good, he will get his reward with his Lord; on such shall be no fear, nor shall they grieve" (Qur'an, 2:112).

Make Allah's pleasure your goal when doing tasks that are difficult for you and your nafs, and remember the job of your nafs is not to make your life easier; rather, it is to frustrate you and your relationship with Allah Almighty. "Surely the nafs incites to evil, except inasmuch as my Lord bestows His mercy" (Qur'an, 12:53).

Moreover, if your spouse is unappreciative, this is no excuse for you to neglect the duties Allah Most High has commanded of you. Showing a lack of appreciation or taking things for granted is improper for any Muslim as seen in this Prophetic saying: "Whoever does not thank people is unthankful to Allah" (Abu Dawud, 4811). This rude and impious habit hinders any relationship, especially the marital one. Feeling gratitude and not showing it is similar to wrapping a gift but not giving it.

As the mother of his children and the maintainer of his private life, it is the duty of the wife to manage both of these with tenderness and discretion. She should remember that her husband, if doing his proper Islamic duty, is sacrificing some of his comfort for her sake and the sake of his children, working hard to provide for her happiness and security.

The Woman's Jihad

*A*LLAH IS MIGHTY AND MAJESTIC. As His servants—males and females, we do things for His pleasure, the way He commands. The duty of a wife, if performed to worship Allah, is as follows:

- "The righteous women are devoutly obedient, and guard in (the husband's) absence what Allah would have them guard" (Qur'an, 4:34).

- "Obey Allah and His Messenger, if you do believe" (Qur'an, 8:1).

- "Whoever submits his whole self to Allah, and is a doer of good, has grasped indeed the most trustworthy hand-hold; and with Allah rests the End and Decision of all affairs" (Qur'an, 31:22).

- "What is with you must vanish: what is with Allah will endure. And We will certainly bestow, on those who patiently persevere, their reward according to the best of their actions" (Qur'an, 16:96).

- "Say: 'My servants who believe fear your Lord. Good is for those who do good in this world... Surely those who patiently persevere will be paid their wages in full without reckoning'" (Qur'an, 39:10).

- "Do you think that you shall enter Paradise without such (trials) as came to those who passed away before you? They encountered suffering and adversity, and were so shaken in spirit that even the Messenger and those of faith who were with him cried: 'When will the help of Allah come?' Ah, but surely the help of Allah is near" (Qur'an, 2:214).

- The Messenger of Allah, Allah bless him and give him peace, was asked which of the women are best. He replied: "The best is she who is pleasing to her husband when he looks at her, who obeys him when he commands her, and who guards for him in his absence both herself and his property" (Nasa'i, 3231).

- The Prophet, Allah bless him and give him peace, said this world is a transitory pleasure and the best pleasure in this world is a righteous woman (Muslim, 2668).

One of the Muslim woman's main obligations after marriage is obedience to her husband. As unpalatable as this idea may seem to those of us raised under the influence of secularism, it is nevertheless a fact of Islamic life.

The Messenger of Allah, Allah bless him and give him peace, said that a woman who obeys her husband and acknowledges his rights is equal to one in jihad (battle) for the sake of Allah Mighty and Majestic. However, few women will actually do this (al-Isti'ab). The Muslim female needs to realize that this is a big part of her jihad (personal struggle) in this world and that success in this jihad is rewarded tremendously.

Obedience to your husband means obeying him in all his lawful requests. The Sacred Law defines what lawful requests are. Those unfamiliar with the legal definition of lawful requests may find it in the books of Islamic jurisprudence (fiqh). The Messenger of Allah, Allah bless him and give him peace, said: "There is no obedience to anyone wherein there is disobedience to Allah" (Ahmad, 1098). It will be easier if you remember that you obey him for Him. If you keep your relationship with Allah, you will never be disappointed.

A wise woman will not quarrel vainly. You should always keep in mind how the devil relishes weaving discord between husband and wife. Do not listen to the advertisements from hell, i.e. the nafs and the devil. The easiest way to create this kind of tension is to make an issue out of every decision. Allah says: "Be steadfast in patience; for verily Allah will not suffer the reward of the righteous to perish" (Qur'an, 11:115). If the husband requires that some things be done in a certain way, it is wise for the wife to obey him, knowing that her obedience to him is in fact obedience to Allah. "You shall certainly be tried and tested in your possessions and in your personal selves... But if you persevere patiently, and guard against evil—surely that is true constancy" (Qur'an, 3:186).

The Messenger of Allah, Allah bless him and give him peace, came as a spiritual guide for both men and women.

He instructed both husband and wife how to behave and sublimate their nafs (lower selves) in regards to the absolute honor and mutual respect they owe each other. The following hadiths should be understood in the context of a real Islamic life where both male and female deserve the honored title of 'Muslim'.

A woman came to the Prophet, Allah bless him and give him peace, for something. After she was finished the Prophet, Allah bless him and give him peace, asked, "Are you married?" She replied, "Yes." He asked, "How do you treat your husband?" She replied, "I do all that is in my capacity." He said, "Look at your relationship with him. Verily, he is your paradise or your hell" (Ahmad, 18524). This means that when she pleases her husband, she has pleased Allah through her obedience to His command. Whereas, when she intentionally upsets him or refuses him, she is incurring Allah's displeasure.

The Messenger of Allah, Allah bless him and give him peace, said: "Allah will not look at a woman that is ungrateful to her husband even though she cannot do without him" (al-Mustadrak, 2771). This is a warning for those women who constantly complain, showing ingratitude to both Allah Most High and their husbands. Lack of contentment is a disease of the heart that ails both men and women. Although this ailment is difficult to eliminate, the consequence of drawing Allah's displeasure upon yourself makes the effort worthwhile.

A woman prepares herself for this struggle by having the knowledge, understanding and will to do what is expected of a Muslim wife. She must realize that it is an ongoing jihad. Allah Most Glorious says: "Of the good that they do, nothing will be rejected of them; for Allah knows well those that do right" (Qur'an, 3:115).

Most important is to make the intention to do everything for Allah. Allah Mighty and Majestic says: "O you who believe, look after your own souls. If you follow guidance, no hurt can come to you from those who stray. The goal of you all is Allah. He will tell you the truth of all that you were doing" (Qur'an, 5:105).

As long as you are aware and continually remind yourself that what you seek is Allah and His pleasure, your tasks, as trying as they may seem, will become easier and the sacrifice they require will be justified. "Allah puts no burden on any person beyond what He has given him. After a difficulty, Allah will soon grant relief" (Qur'an, 65:7).

Healthy Attitude

A BEAUTIFUL AND SUCCINCT summary of the duties of a wife towards her husband is found in the advice Umamah bint al-Harith gave to her daughter who was to be married:

"I'm telling you this not because you are in need of refinement, rather it is a reminder for the unaware and an aid for the wise. Verily my daughter, you are about to leave the common surroundings of your upbringing and go to a new home with a companion you are not familiar with, who has become your overseer. Be a slave to him, he will be a slave to you. Hold fast to these ten things and they will be of service to you:

- Submit to him with contentment.

- Listen well to him and obey.

- Never let his eyes fall on something ugly, be it in your appearance or behavior.

- Never let his nose smell anything from you but a pleasant scent.

- Take care of his sleep time. Do not disturb him, for it will make him angry.

- Take care of his hunger, because the discomfort will make him irritable.

- Take care of his money and manage it well.

- Take care of his children and manage them well.

- Neither ignore his instructions nor divulge his secrets. If you defy his directions, he will hold malice against you. If you disclose his secrets, you will never be safe from his treachery.

- Finally, do not appear elated when you find him disheartened and do not seem depressed when you find him rapturous."

Appearance and Demeanor

THE WIFE MUST TAKE CARE to keep physically clean, take care of her teeth, remove hair from armpits and pubic area, trim her nails, maintain a pleasant smell, and wear clean clothes. These standards of hygiene likewise apply to men, as the lack thereof is repulsive. She should be ready for him to enjoy her, be it looking at her, talking to her, playing or joking with her, or making love with her.

A woman, no matter how physically beautiful, ceases to be so when she behaves improperly. The Messenger of Allah, Allah bless him and give him peace, defined one type of improper behavior: "Among the reasons that the majority in hell are women is their constant cursing, insulting and vilifying" (Bukhari, 304). Moreover, a woman who might not ordinarily be called 'beautiful' becomes so through her tender and loving nature and excellent character.

The Messenger of Allah, Allah bless him and give him peace, said: "No believer benefits from anything after taqwa (God-fearingness) more than he does from a pious wife. If he orders her she obeys; if he looks at her, he is pleased; if he makes an oath, she tries to help him fulfill his word; and if he is absent, she protects herself and his money" (Ibn Majah, 1857).

Trivial matters, like whether to cook beans or broccoli, should not be argued about. Trivial decisions must be made all the time and a man should be above interfering with things that are his wife's domain. You should not waste time arguing about trivialities keeping in mind that almost any situation can be turned into a conflict. Vehemence does not bring good—it brings the opposite. Do not bicker over words.

It takes talent and good demeanor to control yourself and defuse tension. If this crucial skill does not exist, then it must be developed. The ability to defuse tension is the hallmark of a precious wife and wise husband. The Messenger of Allah, Allah bless him and give him peace, said: "Religious women are better than the maidens of paradise" (Tabarani al-Kabir, 23.870).

In shaping your demeanor, you should be grateful for that which Allah Most Generous has given you. It is not always easy to see the mercy or goodness in the situation Allah Mighty and Majestic has placed you in. This contentment grows out of your slavehood to Allah—if you understand this, you are able to worship Him wherever He places you. Surely, 'it is greener on the other side' is an advertisement from the devil and the nafs (lower self).

Everything is from Allah Almighty, and everything is good for the believer. Whether pleased with circumstances or patiently enduring them, in either case, you strive for the pleasure of Allah through your reactions to the situations and things that Allah Most Wise sends you. Our beloved Prophet, Allah bless him and give him peace, has told us, "Strange indeed is the affairs of a believer, for all that happens to him is for the best—and this pertains to none but the believer. If good occurs, he gives thanks (to Allah) and that is best for him. And if difficulty befalls, he remains patient, and that is best for him" (Muslim, 2999).

The Prophet, Allah bless him and give him peace, said, "Look at those less fortunate than yourself, rather than those more fortunate, in order not to be dismissive of the blessings you do have" (Muslim, 2963).

If you do not give thanks for your blessings, you are exposing yourself to the possibility of losing them. Bitterness about what Allah has destined is a sin that wipes out much good and compounds other sins. It prevents you from clearly seeing the blessings and Divine grace contained within your tests and trials; you are also less likely to remember all the other blessings Allah has bestowed upon you such as health and so forth.

Allah Most High says, "Few of My servants are thankful" (Qur'an, 34:13). Are you striving to be among those few?

"Contentment is a treasure inexhaustible" (al-Bayhaqi, 2.88). This vital Islamic characteristic is applicable to all Muslims, young and old, male and female. Having contentment is a precious trait that makes all the unavoidable difficulties in life a little bit easier.

Obedience or Abuse

ALLAH MOST HIGH WARNS: "And those who annoy believing men and believing women undeservedly, bear on themselves a calumny and manifest sin" (Qur'an, 33:58).

Some Muslim husbands believe that wifely obedience entails an obligation to comply with every whim and fancy: if he orders her to stand on one leg or touch her nose, she has to do so. Is this what is meant by obedience? This idiotic attitude is far from Islamic decorum. It is haram (unlawful) to belittle a fellow Muslim. We must look at the essence of obedience in Islam, not merely its form. He who has behaved thus has behaved in a way Allah Mighty and Majestic has forbidden, thus drawing Allah's wrath upon himself. "Fear Allah; for Allah is swift in taking account" (Qur'an, 5:4). Remember that each one of us is a slave of Allah, thus we must have the manners of a slave of Allah i.e. humility.

Heed Allah's advice: "Guard yourselves against a day when one soul shall not avail another nor shall intercession be accepted for it, nor shall compensation be taken from it, nor shall anyone be helped" (Qur'an, 2:48). If you are a steadfast Muslim, then let all who deal with you benefit from your gentleness and generosity.

This is how Allah Most High ordered the Prophet, Allah bless him and give him peace, to behave, "Lower your wing (in gentleness) to the believers" (Qur'an, 15:88). Are you following his exemplary way or not? Islam means submission, and submission takes knowledge, effort and application. If Allah Most Generous has blessed you with obedience and inner peace, give thanks to Him. Run away from the disgrace of disobedience.

The Messenger of Allah, Allah bless him and give him peace, said, "The best of you are those who have the best character [khuluq, which refers to both disposition and behavior]" (Bukhari, 6029). As well as, "There is nothing that weighs more on the Day of Judgment than good character" (Abu Dawud, 4799).

Allah Most High says: "Those who, having done something to be ashamed of, or wronged their own souls, earnestly bring Allah to mind, and ask for forgiveness for their sins; and who can forgive sins except Allah? And are never obstinate in persisting knowingly in the wrong they have done" (Qur'an, 3:135).

The Wife Who Earns Paradise

THE FOLLOWING HADITHS do not mean that the husband should make this trial as difficult as possible for his wife. After all, we are all His servants. As the Messenger of Allah, Allah bless him and give him peace, said, "None of you believes until he loves for his fellow Muslim that which he loves for himself" (Bukhari, 13).

Allah Mighty and Majestic says: "Those who believe and work righteousness, and humble themselves before their Lord, they will be Companions of the Garden, to dwell therein forever" (Qur'an, 11:23).

The Messenger of Allah, Allah bless him and give him peace, said: "A woman who dies, leaving her husband content with her, will enter Paradise" (Tirmidhi, 1161). This assumes that the wife has first and foremost obeyed Allah Most High. There is no benefit in obeying your husband wherein you disobey Allah, Lord of both of you. "If a woman performs the five prayers, fasts Ramadan, does not commit adultery, and obeys her husband, she will be told 'Enter Paradise by any door you wish'" (Ahmad, 1664).

A woman came to the Prophet, Allah bless him and give him peace, and said: "Allah is Lord of men and women, and you are the Messenger of Allah to men and women, Allah has written jihad for men, then if they are triumphant they are rewarded, if they are martyred they are alive with their Lord who provides for them. What is equivalent to their deeds of obedience?" The Prophet, Allah bless him and give him peace, replied: "Obeying your husbands, knowing their rights, and few of you women will do this" (Tabarani al-Kabir, 12163). The wise will take heed of the Prophet's, Allah bless him and give him peace, words: "Few of you women will do this." Being among the elect is never easy, especially when the reward is so great.

The Messenger of Allah, Allah bless him and give him peace, said: "Shall I tell you of your women who earn paradise? She is the tender loving and fertile woman who if she gets angry or is mistreated, or makes her husband angry, will go to him and place her hand in his and say: 'I will not sleep until you are pleased'" (Tabarani al-Saghir, 118). This hadith encourages the wife to be better (because the one who gives 'salams' first is better, *Bukhari*, 5883) than her husband and one of those beloved by Allah Most High and His Messenger, Allah bless him and give him peace, for being kind and forgiving. "Verily, Allah loves those who are kind" (Qur'an, 5:13). "Allah loves those... who forgive whenever they get angry" (Qur'an, 42:37). "And the most beloved of you to me [the Messenger of Allah] are those with the best character" (Bukhari, 3760).

Protocol with In-Laws

DEALING WITH IN-LAWS can be a sensitive issue. From the first six months to a year, most couples are busy adjusting to married life and establishing themselves as a couple within the two families and community.

It is often from the time of the engagement that in-laws start to get hypersensitive to you, the new couple. They may be torn somewhere between separation-anxiety and jealousy; so be aware of their needs for acknowledgement, appreciation and love.

You are falling in love and everyone else fears that you might exclude them from your new life; this usually occurs with the women-folk on the groom's side, particularly his mother. It can also occur with the men-folk on the bride's side, who may be apprehensive now that their baby has grown up and no longer needs them. Of course, these are generalizations that you may not experience in your families.

In addition to their anxiety over the son/daughter moving out and on to a new life without them, jealousy may also arise. It is wise for a new couple to show extra love and concern to those around them during this challenging transition into the new marriage. Share your new happiness with them. Sharing does not mean you must let them run your life or make all the decisions; rather, include them so they feel someone has joined the family and not like someone has been taken away.

If you share your happiness, you will be happy. If you do not share it, your happiness will not last long because of the troubles it will most likely cause with those around you.

If your in-laws have a healthy relationship with their son or daughter, brother or sister, then they will be pleased by your new life and happiness. Most problems are easily solved, as long as they do not feel like you are taking their loved one away from them and that you are willing to share. If you give your spouse the space to have a pleasant relationship with his/her family, it will confirm to the in-laws that you have joined them, rather than depriving them. It will also show them you are not trying to exclude them from your new life.

However, if they do not have a healthy relationship, then this will make your job of pleasing them more difficult. A relative's extreme possessiveness of your spouse is rough for everyone involved. In some situations radical action may be required, while in others, a little adapting is enough. Each situation must be dealt with on its own terms.

Trying to cut your spouse off from their family is unwise and usually causes everyone a lot of pain and resentment.

Give your spouse the liberty and time to socialize with them and do not feel threatened by your spouse's love for them. This type of generosity increases your spouse's love for you and helps your in-laws accept and not feel threatened by you. It takes time for a newcomer to become family, but by your lofty Islamic behavior, it is possible.

Be aware of the mistake many new couples make when, enveloped in love, they turn their backs on other important relationships and abandon their obligations. It is immature to think that all your needs can be met by your spouse and you need no other relationship with parents, siblings, uncles, aunts, friends and so forth. Down the road, this behavior often backfires, leading to unhappiness and isolation. When the sense of completely fulfilling each other wears off and the baraka (blessing) diminishes because of all the broken hearts left by the wayside, you then realize what you have lost. It is natural and healthy that we have good people around us to help us, give us advice, guide us through our difficult times, and to just simply share our lives with. "Blessings are with your elders [righteous, God-fearing and wise]" (Ibn Hibban, 2.319), so do not deprive yourself.

The relationship with the in-laws usually settles down after the new family member has shared a variety of experiences with them. Be patient; it will not happen overnight and it could take as much as ten years or so. When everyone has gotten used to each other, you reap the benefits of the polite norms you set. If you have not established pleasant norms, then you will suffer the unpleasant ones for a long time, perhaps even the rest of your lives.

Another common dilemma is when your family is mean and nasty to your spouse; this usually happens to the bride. How you react to these predicaments, sympathetically or otherwise, often affects your spouse's ability to deal with them.

As Muslims, as parents and children, and as in-laws and spouses, we should always take Allah and His commands seriously, because the consequence of not doing so is disastrous. We can choose to obey Allah and put Him first, subjugate our nafs, close the door on the devil and live a happy life, a life blessed by beautiful Islamic character and manners. Remember, if we behave as Muslims, Allah will put love between our hearts.

"By Him in whose hand is my soul, none of you will enter paradise until you believe, and none of you will believe until you love each other. Shall I not tell you of something which if you do it will create love among you? Increase the custom of greeting each other with 'as-Salamu alaykum'" (Muslim, 54).

Or, we can choose to do the opposite and have a miserable life, in this world and the next, by saying every ugly word that comes to mind and following every wicked plot that the devil whispers in order to cause discord between Muslims. After all, are we all not Muslims? We will live a life in the midst of enemies—perhaps a long life— because of our lack of God-fearingness and un-Islamic behavior. Allah Mighty and Majestic warns:

Whoever holds firmly to Allah shall be guided to a straight path.

O you who believe! Fear Allah as He should be feared, and do not die except in a state of Islam.

And hold fast, all together, by the rope of Allah, and do not divide among yourselves. And remember Allah's favor on you; how you were enemies and He joined your hearts in love, so that you became brothers by His grace; and how you were on the brink of a pit of fire, and He saved you from it. Thus Allah makes plain His signs to you, that you may be guided.

Let there arise out of you a band of people who invite to goodness and enjoin what is right, and forbid what is wrong. Such are the ones who attain felicity.

Do not be of those who are divided amongst themselves and fall into disputations after receiving clear signs. For them is a dreadful punishment.

On the day when some faces will be bright, and some faces blackened, it will be said: 'Did you reject faith after accepting it? Taste then the penalty for rejecting faith.'

As for those whose faces will be bright, they will be in Allah's mercy—therein to dwell forever.

These are the signs of Allah. We recite them to you in truth. And Allah wills no injustice to any of His creatures.

Whatever is between the heavens and earth belong to Allah. To Him all things return (Qur'an, 3:101-109).

Your spouse can endure many annoyances from the in-laws as long as your spouse feels that you recognize and appreciate the hardship they are going through for your sake in order to keep the peace. "If you have patience and fear Allah, their guile will never harm you. Allah is surrounding what they do" (Qur'an, 3:120). However, your spouse's patience can run out if you do not acknowledge, appreciate and sympathize with the injustices they are tolerating. Your lack of acknowledgement often causes a sense of bitterness, isolation and insecurity for your spouse. Under these circumstances, if you do not empathize with your spouse, who will?

Even if you do not really understand what your spouse may be experiencing or you believe they are just imagining problems with your family, it is better to show sympathy to help them through it. If you show sympathy, it is more likely that they will be willing to consider your advice or point of view. If you are unsympathetic, then your spouse will accuse you of taking your family's side. This can cause an ongoing sense of bitterness that your spouse will find very difficult to forgive and forget.

These problems with the in-laws commonly happen with your spouse, but they could happen with anyone else in your family. In either case, handle the situation the same, i.e. with understanding. If one side is unacceptably out of line, then responsible measures need to be taken. You are obliged to prohibit the wrong and stand firm for what is fair and right.

Allah Most High says, "They believe in Allah and the Last Day, and enjoin what is right and forbid what is evil, and vie with one another in good works. They are the righteous. And whatever good they do, its reward will not be denied them. Allah is Aware of those who are righteous" (Qur'an 3:114-15).

It is best for the husband to deal with his family and for the wife to deal with hers if there are sensitive issues or problems. This is generally true but there might be situations that are exceptions.

Showdowns often cause irreconcilable damage. Always keep a cool head when dealing with in-laws. It is easier for family members to forgive each other than to forgive an outsider.

And everyone should keep in mind, "If Allah helps you, none can overcome you. If He abandons you, who then can help you? In Allah let believers put their trust" (Qur'an, 3:160).

"Can one who seeks the pleasure of Allah be compared to him who has incurred the wrath of Allah? Hell shall be their habitation. Evil shall be their fate" (Qur'an, 3:162).

Our beloved Prophet, Allah bless him and give him peace, said, "The disease of [previous] nations has crept up upon you: envy and hatred. Truly, hatred is a shaver; it shaves away not hair, but religion. By Him in whose hand is my soul, you shall not enter paradise until you believe. And you shall not believe until you love one another (Musnad al-Bazzar, 6.192:2232).

4

Staying Married
Integrals of Success

Good and bad marriages are made;
neither one comes by chance

Allah Mighty and Majestic says,

And of His signs is that He created for you,
of yourselves, spouses, that you may dwell
in tranquility with them, and
He has set between you
love and mercy.
Surely in that are signs for a people who reflect
(Qur'an, 30:21)

And those who annoy
believing men and believing women undeservedly,
bear on themselves a calumny and manifest sin
(Qur'an, 33:58)

Speak gently and politely with one another...do not defame
nor be sarcastic to each other, nor call each other by
offensive nicknames;
ill seeming is a name connoting wickedness
to be used of one after he has believed
and those who do not desist
are indeed doing wrong
(Qur'an, 49:11)

O mankind, We have created you male and female ...
that you may know one another.
Surely the noblest among you in the sight of Allah
is the most God-fearing of you
(Qur'an, 49:13)

Preconceptions

WHEN SPARKS DO NOT fly during the first kiss and violins do not play when you embrace, do not fear that this is not a match made in heaven. These things only happen in Hollywood movies. In Islam, love grows after marriage, and usually it is only after experiencing your spouse's pious behavior that love begins to strengthen.

These Hollywood expectations often put a lot of unnecessary stress on a relationship. It deludes you into thinking that if there is no magic feeling, then this surely cannot be the marriage for you. In movies, the actors fake these feelings, and with the appropriate music and background, make you believe that for love to be true, this is how it must be. Not only is this a distortion, but many of these same actors have rotten love lives because they too cannot find it.

One of the major problems this may cause is the attitude of just being partially committed to your marriage and your spouse: one foot in the marriage and the other foot out, ready to leave at the drop of a hat. If this occurs, it is very difficult to get the marriage moving in the right direction, because one or both of you becomes afraid to express your emotions and exert the effort needed to make it work. This leads to many problems and usually causes a very unhappy married life.

Just as the Hollywood romance does not really exist, there is no 'ideal-life-brochure' where you can choose from its catalog and order the life you have always visualized in your mind's eye. Expect misunderstandings, conflicts, anger, miscommunications and misinterpretations during the first couple of years of marriage. These are all normal and not necessarily indications of the end of the marriage, but of living in the real world. In any of these circumstances, the Sacred Law should be your guiding light to how to behave. Avoiding these occurrences is nearly impossible. These situations must be firmly kept in check with what is beautiful Islamic decorum. You should not get frustrated when the marriage does not fit your preconceived or misconceived ideal. With prayer, insight, forbearance, diplomacy, persistent effort, communication, altruism and forgiveness, the relationship you want can come about. With just a little wisdom and a lot of work, you can develop the relationship you hoped for.

People usually do not change after one, two, or even several quarrels. If things are not the way you want, then think of constructive ways to make them better. For example, your spouse always forgets—and it probably drives them crazy just as much as it does you. Instead of fighting for the sake of fighting, displaying anger, frustration or disappointment, try finding practical solutions for the problem. Why not put a 'post it' on the door of the fridge or on the dashboard of the car of the thing or things you want, or anywhere else you think it may help?

If you do not solve your problems, they go on and do not resolve themselves. Hoping for them to go away usually does not work either. Unsolved problems can become a hidden source of other troubles. Finding a solution is how problems get resolved. If you do not know how to go about solving your problems, then ask a specialist for advice. There are some special cases where the passing of time can solve some problems, but these situations are the rare exception. So take the issues at hand—one by one, not all at once—and with beautiful Islamic manners, gracefully proceed to solving them.

If you are spending most of your time fighting, you need to stop doing what you are doing: it is not working. Take a break and assess what is happening. It is foolish to repeatedly do the same thing and expect a different result. Stop doing the things that do not work and look for another solution: either you take positive action or things will remain the same, if they do not get worse.

Through the stages of getting to know each other there are bound to be foreseen and unforeseen problems. It is important to resolve each problem by reaching some type of mutual agreement or understanding. An argument where everyone has had their say may not be communication; it is usually just expressing anger. After the argument, communication starts when you rationally discuss the matter and reach a conclusion, understanding or agreement. The discussion may have to go through several rounds; after the first round if you are not satisfied then a second round, and so forth until you reach some type of conclusion together.

Leaving problems unresolved is unhealthy. However, this does not mean that every problem has to be solved immediately. Do not expect to always finish everything in one sitting. This takes maturity and wisdom on the part of both partners. Fighting and expressing your anger is not very difficult; going beyond this takes God-fearingness, maturity, understanding, diplomacy, commitment and an abundance of forgiveness. Finding solutions or solving problems, if done to please Allah, is worship.

The obsession to tell every aspect of the truth as you perceive it—regardless of the cost—is more often part of the problem rather than part of the solution, when silence or discretion would be much wiser. "Whoever believes in Allah and the Last Day, let him say what is good or remain silent" (Bukhari, 6110).

You have communicated when a problem has been resolved—before that is all wrestling of the nafs (ego). You are always held accountable (see Fallacies about Happiness). Even if you do not feel accountable in front of your spouse, you are accountable to Allah Almighty. Do not take this life too seriously, but take Allah and His commands seriously.

Protect yourself and your family by not listening to the advertisements from hell i.e. from the nafs and devil to spur problems on—have patience. Patience is worship, when you are upset, have the patience to hold that hard nasty word on the tip of your tongue or to put a stop to that aggressive improper behavior. Allah loves piety as well as gentleness. The Messenger of Allah, Allah bless him and give him peace, said: "Verily, Allah loves gentleness in all matters" (Bukhari, 5565).

"O you who believe! Fear Allah, and believe in His Messenger, and He will bestow on you a double portion of His mercy: He will provide for you a light by which you shall walk (straight in you path), and He will forgive you: for Allah is All-forgiving, Most Merciful" (Qur'an, 57:28).

We are obliged to fulfill our duties to Allah—one of our utmost important duties is to change when we know we are doing something wrong. There are two ways to change and improve. The first is being able to understand that a message or advice is from Allah, thus you take heed and make amends to your mistaken ways. This is the easy way. The latter is to wait until Allah sends you a backbreaking trial and you have no other choice but to change. This is the difficult way.

Amongst one of today's worst addictions is the addiction to adrenaline. The problem with this addiction is that the addict is completely unaware of it. Those who become addicted to the effects of the over-stimulation of adrenaline may find that they are in constant need of excitement and excessive activity. It is most likely that the spouse of the

116

adrenaline addict cannot maintain these high demands and often prefers to live a 'normal' life. For the addict everything in life becomes boring when not in a state of stimulation or not 'living on the edge'.

Unfortunately the major consequences of this addiction is that sharing a normal life with one's spouse, or having normal healthy sex with one's spouse, becomes unexciting shortly into the marriage. In fact, life itself becomes dull, anything that is not extremely stimulating is tedious, causing one to feel that there must be something wrong with one's life, one's marriage, one's sex life, as well as anything and everything else. When this happens the boredom can develop into frustration which may become manifest through unreasonable and unjustified levels of anger, fear, anxiety, guilt or worry. Such characteristics become difficult for both partners in the marriage to live with and thus problems begin and escalate. But in fact there is nothing wrong with life or one's marriage—it is merely that you have become hooked on adrenaline, and so see reality from a highly distorted perspective, to the point of normal life becoming abnormal, and abnormality becoming one's normality. So, before one throws away all that is good and healthy in one's life, one should wonder: is it the adrenaline kick that is deceiving me?

Setting the Tone: the Spirit of an Islamic Marriage

ALLAH MOST MERCIFUL SAYS: "They [women] are a garment for you [men] and you are a garment for them" (Qur'an, 2:187). This clearly defines the Islamic marriage as a spiritually reciprocal relationship that covers, supports, and protects you. Ibn 'Abbas explained the verse as a wife being a 'dwelling place of warmth, love and security' for her husband just as a husband is for her (Ibn Kathir).

Positive daily reinforcement is essential to maintaining a stable, harmonious tone in the relationship. Like a well-kept garden, marriage takes both love and effort each day to keep it flourishing. Good marriages are made—they do not just happen. The primary key to this is simply being kind and respectful to each other. As basic as this may sound, it is often lacking in faulty marriages.

In some, you find that the marital contract has become a license for the spouses to assuage their own egos (nafs). In others, you find each spouse keeps score of the ongoing feud, taking every opportunity to get the better of the 'enemy'. This, as well as all other types of appalling behavior between Muslim spouses, is tragic, not only for those involved but for the whole Islamic community. A relationship subject to mercurial moods and unsettled arguments is poor material for an Islamic marriage.

It is important for us to observe our emotions while not reacting to or being controlled by them. Control them instead of being controlled by them. Learning to use your emotions to think—not thinking with your emotions—is very important before and after marriage. Many do not realize that their emotions do their thinking for them. Handling emotions, delaying reactions and thinking clearly is a sign of maturity. Being in control of—not controlled by—your emotions is intelligence. Mastering this will be instrumental for you in dealing with marriage problems as well as all other problems in life.

An Islamic marriage is one from which each partner derives love, strength, affection, and security; all of which assist you in your journey to Allah. Each partner must be in a constant jihad (personal struggle) against the devil and their own nafs (lower self), to prevent the entry of any poison into their marriage. Allah Mighty and Majestic says: "If any do deeds of righteousness—be they male or female— and have faith, they will enter Heaven, and not the least injustice will be done to them" (Qur'an, 4:124).

The spirit of an Islamic marriage is one of husband and wife trying to gently pull each other into paradise. This requires that both conduct themselves as good Muslims, tenderly encouraging each other to do what pleases Allah. Each partner should constantly keep in mind the struggles of the other and do their best to create the atmosphere most conducive to seeking the pleasure of Allah.

Sometime your spouse does not want to hear the truth; they just want and need your support and love. In order to have a friend you must be one. Vices such as anger, sarcasm, and selfishness are a hindrance to a solid, stable relationship in the path of Allah, Mighty and Majestic. Allah Most Gracious commands believers to: "Speak gently and politely with one another... do not defame nor be sarcastic to each other, nor call each other by offensive nicknames; ill seeming is a name connoting wickedness to be used of one after he has believed and those who do not desist are indeed doing wrong" (Qur'an, 49:11).

The good manners that are required of an individual are much more imperative in marriage. It is said there are three qualities found in a friend of Allah: if given anything, he is grateful; if he has the power to avenge, he forgives; and if he gets angry, he controls himself and calms down.

After the Big Step—Marriage and the Nafs

SPIRITUAL STRUGGLE (jihad al-nafs) is truly something done solely for the pleasure of Allah. If you are already married, you may have found that marriage can be a real means of spiritual struggle. Perhaps before marriage, your jihad was lacking in some ways, and marriage has given you a greater opportunity to work on it.

It is the nature of marriage and the constant contact with your partner that often provokes your nafs. Marriage is definitely the place where the nafs of each spouse comes face to face—and what happens after that is up to you. If you can behave properly toward other people, then you should be able to behave your best towards your partner.

Marriage is not a license for a man or woman to unleash their nafs on their spouse. Rather it is a license for them to live together in love and tranquility. Allah Most High says: "And those who strive in Our cause, We will certainly guide them in Our ways: verily Allah is with those who do right" (Qur'an, 29:69). The spiritual way is not only moving forward by spiritual works, but also keeping from stumbling back by avoiding actions that hinder our spiritual progress and open the door for Satan.

It is the devil's way to encourage strife between Muslims. Comparing your own circumstances with those of your relatives, friends, neighbors or other Muslims is generally a source of ingratitude and envy, both of which are haram (forbidden) and well-recognized diseases of the heart. They are unsuited for a believer and must be cured (for details see Appearance and Demeanor above).

"Beware of envy, for envy consumes good works as fire consumes wood" (Abu Dawud, 4903).

Allah Most High says, "In no way covet those things in which Allah has bestowed His gifts more freely on some of you than on others: To men is allotted what they earn, and to women what they earn; but ask Allah of His bounty. For Allah has full knowledge of all things" (Qur'an, 4:32).

Allah Most Generous has given everyone his or her own particular circumstances—if seen in the correct perspective all are opportunities to draw nearer to Him. When one is constantly complaining, comparing, and nagging it leads to useless and endless arguing. There is much wisdom in the Arabic proverb: "Complaining to anyone other than Allah is degrading."

Allah Mighty and Majestic says: "If Allah touches you with affliction, none can remove it but He; if He touch you with happiness, He has power over all things" (Qur'an, 6:17).

Ask the One who can respond to your grievances: "Call upon Me and I will answer you" (Qur'an, 40:60).

Establishing Good Habits

ℱROM THE BEGINNING of the relationship, good habits are crucial. Successful marriages are built and refined with the help of good habits established from the beginning. The damage done by bad habits and unacceptable behavior takes an immense amount of effort to rectify and is often irrevocable. As with anything else in this world, a good job the first time is infinitely superior to a patched-up second try. Do not wait for a good marriage: unless you make it, it will never happen.

During the first few years of marriage, a mutual effort is necessary to establish the kinds of habits that will last throughout the marriage. Love does not mean seeing everything eye to eye, or feeling or thinking the same way in every matter—love entails the maturity to respect differences.

Idiosyncrasies must be discovered and assimilated into the relationship. It is the duty of each spouse to discover the strengths and weaknesses of their partner and act accordingly. Neither should expect the other to be aware of all his or her sensitive areas.

The misconception that your spouse should know, understand and react to every aspect of your personality is a grave mistake. Before saying to yourself: "He should know that about me," or "She knows that makes me angry," or "I've told him before, he's just trying to make me mad," you should take the time to gently explain again to your partner whatever you feel they should know, in order to make the relationship function more smoothly. Conversely, you ought to listen attentively to your partner and learn to be considerate. A principle of Islam is to take oneself to task first. A "little" thing to you could be a major annoyance to your partner. Often the "little" things irritate a great deal hence require ample care.

Similarly, presuming to know exactly what your partner is feeling or thinking or how your partner will act or react is another grave mistake. Naturally, you can observe signs of your partner's feelings and, with time, generally know what they think about things and how they might react to things. However, the problem is in your insisting that you know what your partner feels and thinks and how they will react. Omniscience belongs to Allah alone, so it is best left with Him. Busying yourself searching for your partner's failings is a clear invitation from the devil.

Many marriages break down because of lack of skill or timing in communicating. Individuals often believe they are expressing themselves clearly but find that the problem remains. You should not assume your spouse understands you; if ever in doubt, talk it out.

A basic moral quality expected of a Muslim is to have a good opinion of his fellow Muslims and to give them the benefit of the doubt. In practice, this means that if you are upset and unable to assume the best, then, after calming down, discuss the matter thoroughly. These dunya (worldly) matters should be taken lightly as it is their nature to be a trial. "That which is on earth We have made but as a glittering show for the earth, in order that We may test them, as to which of them are best in conduct" (Qur'an, 18:7). Let the problems of the dunya pass but hold seriously to the things that matter in the hereafter—your obedience or disobedience to Allah's commands.

Self-sacrifice and humility are invaluable provisions in striving to set the tone for an Islamic marriage. People today, especially those who were raised in the West, are so used to constantly demanding their rights that they bring this attitude into their marriages as well. Such behavior in a marriage leads to a brinkmanship between egos in which both parties inevitably lose. It is easier to take than to give—however, giving rather than taking is a major ingredient to a happy marriage.

Good Humor

$\mathcal{A}$ SENSE OF HUMOR is one of the most essential aspects of a healthy relationship. It is invaluable in dealing with and overcoming difficult situations. Without it, minor inconveniences or unexpected circumstances become needlessly difficult. With it, difficult challenges are transformed into a chance for husband and wife to grow closer by being a respite from the stress.

The ability to laugh things off and take things lightly relieves a great deal of pressure and makes patience in adversity much easier. Let your fellow Muslim, your spouse, benefit from your fine Islamic character. For example, a husband comes home to find that his dinner has been burnt. If he encounters the situation graciously with a light-hearted sense of humor, the already distressed wife will immensely appreciate it. In this case, the husband will have pleased not only his wife, but also his Lord for restraining his anger and relieving a fellow Muslim. "Is there any reward for goodness other than goodness?" (Qur'an, 55:60).

While on the contrary, if he meets the situation with anger or sarcasm, it will only make things worse. The Messenger of Allah, Allah bless him and give him peace, warned, "He who has no compassion for others is not entitled to it from Allah" (Bukhari, 7376).

All humans make mistakes. You can hardly demand perfection when you yourself are not perfect. Tension usually generates tension. Meanness brings no good—it breeds the opposite, whereas a pleasant sense of humor nearly always opens the door of love and compassion.

Sarcasm is by no means what is meant here as a sense of humor. Sarcasm is not the way of Muslims. Sarcasm causes resentment and hurt feelings; good humor encourages warmth and links the hearts together. Kind words mean so much, cost so little and bring much in return.

The benefits of a relationship woven with a light hearted playfulness are both instantaneous and far-reaching. There is a tangible difference between a marriage in which each spouse is aware of how truly insignificant most things are and does not get worked up over everything that does not go as planned, compared to a marriage in which each spouse allows pride or bad temperament to govern.

A positive change in your attitude can alter your life completely. Like any other good habit, maintaining a good sense of humor in difficult circumstances may take time until it becomes natural. You may need to remind yourself and your spouse of its importance and consciously resolve to establish it in your marriage. This attitude conforms to the way of Islam, as you understand that this life is transient and what happens to you is only that which Allah has decreed. And what Allah decrees is best, although the nafs (lower self) may not agree.

Getting Along

$\mathcal{T}$AKE A MOMENT TO THINK of what it means to be a Muslim. Then consider these words of Allah Mighty and Majestic along with the words of His Messenger, Allah bless him and give him peace,:

- "And make not your own hands contribute to your destruction; but do good; for Allah loves those who do good" (Qur'an, 2:195).

- "Undoubtedly, Allah knows what they conceal, and what they reveal: Verily He loves not the arrogant" (Qur'an, 16:23).

- "And he who disobeys Allah and His Messenger and transgresses His limits, will be admitted to a fire, to abide there forever and he will have a humiliating punishment" (Qur'an, 4:14).

- "O you who believe! Follow not Satan's footsteps: for whosoever follows the footsteps of Satan, assuredly he commands to indecency and dishonor ... and Allah is All-hearing, All-knowing" (Qur'an, 24:21).

- "Who is better in speech than one who calls men to Allah, works righteousness, and says: 'Surely I am a Muslim.' Not equal are goodness and evil. Repel evil with what is better and behold: he between whom and you was enmity become as if he were your loyal friend. And no one will be granted such goodness except those who exercise patience and self-restraint, none but persons of the greatest good fortune. And if at anytime an incitement to discord is made to you by the devil, seek refuge in Allah. He is the One who hears and knows all things" (Qur'an, 41:33-6).

- "The recompense for an injury is an injury equal thereto (in degree): but if a person forgives and makes reconciliation, his reward is due from Allah: for (Allah) loves not those who do wrong. But indeed, if any do help and defend themselves after a wrong (done) to them, against such there is no cause of blame. The blame is only against those who oppress men with wrongdoing and insolently transgress beyond bounds through the land, defying right and justice: for such there will be a Penalty grievous. But indeed if any show patience and forgive, that would truly be an exercise of courageous will and resolution in the conduct of affairs" (Qur'an, 42:40-3).

- "Prayer is light, charity is a proof; patience is illumination; and the Qur'an is an argument for or against you.

Everyone starts his day and is a vendor of his soul, either freeing it or bringing about its ruin" (Muslim, 223).

- "One who shows no mercy will be shown no mercy [by Allah]" (Bukhari, 6013).

- "A servant thoughtlessly says something pleasing to Allah Most High for which Allah raises him whole degrees. And a servant thoughtlessly says something detested by Allah Most High for which he plunges into hell" (Bukhari, 6113).

- "The best of you are the best to his wife, and I am the best of you to my wives" (Tirmidhi, 3895).

Marriage is a lifelong commitment. We have to view our spouses as companions through our journey of life. If we keep this and the Prophetic example in mind, our differences and problems should be overcome with gentleness and patience. Guided by the Prophetic example in the words of Allah Most High: "We have not sent you [Muhammad], but as a mercy unto the worlds" (Qur'an, 21:107).

Differences should be resolved with wisdom and patience. It is good advice not to go to sleep until your heart is clear toward your spouse. You can achieve this by having frank but tactful communication, with patience and wisdom. Shun arrogance and keep in mind that it could be you who is wrong.

When communicating, it is necessary to be flexible, not stubborn: anything permissible your spouse asks of you should be considered. To do all the talking and none of the listening is an ugly form of greed and selfishness. You must listen to your spouse's point of view. Be willing to give, not merely take in your relationship. If there is no benevolence, there is discord. It could be that your spouse may be having a bad day, and instead of insisting on your personal issue or understanding, try to be empathetic. There is nothing like loving kindness to smooth over the bumps.

Allah Most High says: "And of His signs is that He created for you, of yourselves, spouses, that you may dwell in tranquility with them, and He has set between you love and mercy. Surely in that are signs for a people who reflect" (Qur'an, 30:21).

The Qur'anic concept of marriage is characterized by love, mercy and tranquility, not by possession, domination and highhandedness. Imagine yourself on a small boat, trying to cross a vast ocean, with your sole companion being your spouse. If you keep fighting and arguing, your boat will drift aimlessly, if not capsize. You have no option but to work things out and cooperate in your life-journey. This life is short; you need not make it miserable.

When you help others, you often are helping yourself. And this is especially true if the other is your spouse. Allah Most High says: "What is the life of this world but play and diversion? But best is the home in the Hereafter, for those who are righteous. Will you not then understand?" (Qur'an, 6:32).

When problems do occur, you should not make it a habit to discuss them with anyone and everyone. Many well-meaning advisors give horrible and wrong advice. Advice should be sought only from those qualified to give it.

From the chapter on 'Holding One's Tongue' in Nawawi's *al-Adhkar*: Arguing is importunateness in speech to gain one's end, whether monetary or other. It may be initiated by oneself or in response to another. If one objects that a person must argue to obtain his rights, the reply is that the stern condemnation of it applies to those who argue without right or knowledge, or someone who adds abuse to his speech that is not necessary to secure his rights, or is motivated to argue by nothing besides an obstinate desire to win and to finish his opponent. As for someone who has been wronged and makes his case in a way compatible with the Sacred Law, without belligerence, excessiveness, or importunateness, and not intending more obstinacy and abuse, it is not unlawful, though it is better to avoid it if there is any way to do so, for keeping one's tongue within the limits of fair play during the course of an argument is virtually impossible. Moreover, arguing produces rancor in hearts and causes animosity that can lead to actual hatred between two people, until each comes to be pleased when harm befalls the other and to be displeased at the good, and unleashes his tongue against the other's reputation. Whoever argues runs the risk of these calamities. At the minimum, a quarrel comes to preoccupy one's heart so that during the prayer one's thoughts turn to debating and arguing, and one does not remain as on should. A certain person remarked, "I have not seen anything that impairs one's religion, diminishes one's respectability, ends one's happiness, or preoccupies one's heart like arguing" (*Reliance of the Traveller*, 758-59).

Dealing with Problems

WITH THE PREVIOUS QUR'ANIC VERSES and hadiths in mind, consider the following as part of your criterion for solving problems:

- "O you who believe! If you fear Allah, He will grant you a criterion (to judge between right and wrong), and acquit you of your evil deeds, and forgive you; for Allah is the Lord of grace unbounded" (Qur'an, 8:29).

- "Is he who is on the true Guidance from his Lord to be compared with him whose evil conduct seems pleasing to him and who follow his own lusts" (Qur'an, 47:14)?

- "Serve Allah, and join not any partners with Him; and do good to ... the companion by your side... for Allah loves not the arrogant, the vainglorious" (Qur'an, 4:36).

- "Is it that there is a disease in their hearts? Or do they doubt, or are they in fear, that Allah and His Messenger will deal unjustly with them? Nay, it is they themselves who do wrong. The answer of the believers, when summoned to Allah and His Messenger, in order that he may judge between them, is no other than this: they say, 'We hear and we obey': it is such as these that will attain felicity. It is such as obey Allah and His Messenger, and fear Allah and do right, they are the triumphant" (Qur'an, 24:50-2).

- "Not equal are the corrupt and the good ... so fear Allah, O you who understand" (Qur'an, 5:100).

- "Those who show patience and constancy, and work righteousness; for them is forgiveness and a great reward" (Qur'an, 11:11).

- "Obey Allah and His Messenger; and do not quarrel together, so that you lose heart and your power departs; and be patient and persevering: for Allah is with those who patiently persevere" (Qur'an, 8:46).

- "Invite to the Way of your Lord with wisdom and beautiful preaching; and argue with them in ways that are best and most gracious: for your Lord knows best, who have strayed from His Path, and who receive guidance" (Qur'an, 16:125).

- "And servants of the All-merciful are those who walk on the earth in humility, and when the ignorant address them, they say, 'Peace'" (Qur'an, 25:63).

- "Surely Allah is never unjust in the least degree: if it be a good deed He will double it, and gives from Himself a great reward" (Qur'an, 4:40).

- "Allah loves not the evildoers" (Qur'an, 3:140).

- "Like those who a short time before them tasted the mischief of their action; there awaits them a painful chastisement. Like Satan, when he said to man,

'Disbelieve'; then, when he disbelieved, he said, 'Surely I am free of you. Surely, I fear Allah, the Lord of the Worlds'. The end of both will be in the Fire, there dwelling forever; that is the recompense of the evil doers. O you who believe, fear Allah. Let every soul consider what it has forwarded for the morrow. And fear Allah; Allah is aware of the things you do. Be not as those who forgot Allah, and so He caused them to forget their souls; such are the ungodly. Not equal are the inhabitants of the Fire and the inhabitants of Paradise. The inhabitants of Paradise—they are the triumphant" (Qur'an, 59:15-20).

- Whoever has the following four characteristics will be a pure hypocrite and whoever has one of the following four characteristics will have one characteristic of hypocrisy unless and until he gives it up:

  [1.] When he is entrusted with something, he betrays the trust;

  [2.] When he speaks he lies;

  [3.] When he makes a covenant, he proves to be treacherous;

  [4.] When he quarrels, he behaves in a very imprudent, evil and insulting manner (Bukhari, 34).

- "Let there be no harming or reciprocating harm" (Ibn Majah, 2340).

- "Gentleness is not found in anything except that it beautifies it, and gentleness is not taken from anything except that it disfigures it" (Muslim, 2594).

- "Righteousness is good character, and sin is that which wavers in your soul and which you dislike people finding out about" (Muslim, 2253).

- "A believer is not given to reviling, cursing, vulgarity or obscenity" (Ibn Hibban, 192).

As marriage is a fusion of two imperfect elements, it is inevitable that problems arise and tempers flare. These displays do not mean that the marriage is in peril. Rather, it is the way in which anger is handled that shows both wisdom and strength or the lack thereof. Islamic decorum is called for at all times. "Allah is with those who restrain themselves" (Qur'an, 9:36). And remember: "Allah loves those who are patient" (Qur'an, 3:146).

Allowing yourself to be overcome by the argument or your anger means that the aftermath will be ever more difficult to rectify. Arguments are inevitable, but what usually leaves indelible scars is not the subject of the argument itself, but rather the ugliness with which it is handled.

There is no excuse for allowing yourself to unleash unforgivable words or actions on your spouse. Your partner may not forget as quickly as you do—especially when you tap a nerve that the slightest touch hurts.

People who have a problem controlling their anger often 'go for the jugular vein' when they argue with their spouse, or anyone else for that matter. Instead of discussing the problem, they often end up doing a partial or complete 'character assassination' of their opponent. This naturally makes the attacked person defensive and usually causes them to just tune out and shut the attacker out. This behavior is repulsive and un-Islamic, while at the same time very detrimental to the relationship—wiping out any form of communication. Hurting your spouse normally does not change them in the way you want; rather, it causes resentment.

The Prophet, Allah bless him and give him peace, said: "Modesty is of faith, and faith is in paradise. Vulgarity is of rudeness, and rudeness is in hell" (Hakim, 171).

It is crucial for each partner to constantly keep in mind that this endeavor is one of the most important jihads (personal struggles) of their life and that Allah Mighty and Majestic is ever watchful of how you conduct yourself. "O believers, fear Allah. Let every soul consider what it has forwarded for the morrow. And fear Allah; Allah is well acquainted with what you do" (Qur'an, 59:18).

Allah Most Gracious says: "The believers indeed are brethren, so reconcile your two brethren" (Qur'an, 49:10). Remind yourself that there is a relationship of Islamic brotherhood with your spouse above and beyond your marital relationship.

Stubbornness and insisting that you take your rights at all costs and on every occasion may be gratifying to your nafs (ego) at first, but will quickly make for a confrontational relationship. "If a suggestion from Satan assails you, seek refuge with Allah; for He is All-hearing and All-knowing" (Qur'an, 7:200). And if you persist in gratifying your nafs, then consider these words of Allah: "When the suffering reached them from Us, why then did they not learn humility? On the contrary their hearts became hardened, and Satan made their (sinful) acts seem alluring to them" (Qur'an, 6:43).

Your marriage as a whole should be more important than always getting your way. It is better for you to be happy than always right. If you win and your relationship loses, then you have actually lost. Is it worth it? You must keep in mind the long-term consequences of this ugly behavior on your marriage as well as your life.

Too often, you come across husbands and wives who have completely lost any semblance of friendship that they may once have had. This is often because in the reality of living with one another, the darker side of the nafs shows its ugly face, be it in the form of a grotesque fit of rage or other unseemly behavior. The spouse then reacts to this display in a way that he or she feels entitled, and the battle begins. Surely, this is a conflict in which neither party will be the victor. "Help one another in righteousness and piety, but help not one another in sin and rancor: fear Allah, for Allah is strict in punishment" (Qur'an, 5:2).

What lies in your strength to do, lies in your strength not to do. You must always keep in mind that you may be destined to remain with your spouse for a long time—perhaps a lifetime. Considering that this means a daily relationship in which children may be a part, the last thing you want is to live with an enemy. Never underestimate how detrimental a bad marriage is for children. What will you do if because of the lack of implying beautiful Islamic etiquette in your life one or all of your children leaves Islam saying it did not work for my parents and did not help our lives? And if the children do not leave Islam then often the scars of a bad marriage can affect them for the rest of their lives; the lack of good role models and an unstable family life causes a lot of insecurity in the children and a poor conception of how a happy family should function. Failure is not from lack of strength and ability; rather it is from lack of willpower and wisdom. This failure destroys many lives because of the parental lack of realization of the consequences of their actions.

In general, you need to be moderate and avoid excesses in your emotions, especially anger. Excessive anger is an illness that must be cured. The Messenger of Allah, Allah bless him and give him peace, said, "Anger is from the Devil. The Devil was made from fire. What puts out fire is water, so if one of you gets angry he should perform ablution" (Abu Dawud, 4784).

He, Allah bless him and give him peace, also instructed us, "If one of you gets angry, he should say: 'A'ûdhu bi Llâhi min ash-shaytân ar-rajîm (I seek refuge in Allah from the accursed Devil) and his anger should then leave him" (Bukhari, 3282).

In addition: "If one of you gets angry and is standing, let him sit down. The anger should then go away; if not, he should lay down" (Ahmad, 20841).

We should look to the Messenger of Allah, Allah bless him and give him peace, as he never let his anger make him behave unjustly. He, Allah bless him and give him peace, said, "The strong is not he who possesses physical strength, but rather he who possesses self-control in the face of anger" (Bukhari, 6114).

Suleiman ibn Surad narrated that while he was sitting with the Prophet, Allah bless him and give him peace, two men were exchanging insults and the face of one of them became red with rage, and his jugular veins swelled.

On that the Prophet, Allah bless him and give him peace, said: "Verily, I know a word, if he would say it, it would cause the anger to leave him. If he says: 'A'ûdhu bi Llâhi min ash-shaytân (I seek refuge in Allah from the shaytan). Then all his anger would go away."

Someone told the angry man, "The Prophet, Allah bless him and give him peace, has said, 'Seek refuge with Allah from shaytan'."

The angry man replied, "Am I crazy?"

[He did not want to hear or apply the guidance of the Prophet, Allah bless him and give him peace. May all of us seek refuge in Allah Mighty and Majestic from being someone who does not want to hear and apply guidance from the Prophet, Allah bless him and give him peace.] (Bukhari, 3040).

The Messenger of Allah, Allah bless him and give him peace, also declared, "Whoever controls his raging anger while he has the authority and ability to carry it out, Allah will fill him with security and faith" (Abu Dawud, 4777).

As Abu Darda' advised his wife (Allah be well pleased with them), "If you see me angry, then please me. If I see you angry, I will please you. Otherwise, we will never be reconciled."

Jalal al-Din al-Rumi wrote in his *Mathnawi*, "Let us implore Allah to help us to self-control: one who lacks self-control is deprived of the grace of the Lord. The undisciplined man does not maltreat himself alone, but he sets the whole world on fire."

"O you who believe! Obey Allah and His Messenger, and turn not away from him when you hear him speak. Nor be like those who say, 'We hear,' but listen not. Surely the worst of beasts in the sight of Allah are those who are deaf and dumb, and do not understand" (Qur'an, 8:20-2).

Stability and the Sacred Law

WHEN THERE IS STABILITY in your life, you are ready and able to progress in other things, as in drawing closer to Allah. Live a life that encourages you to love each other for the sake of Allah and let your spouse's idiosyncrasies pass by. Life is trying enough without having to cope with misery you can avoid. The whole Sacred Law and Islamic way of life is designed to create an outward environment and inward state that make spiritual advancement possible.

The application of Islam is not a few chosen sentences out of fiqh (Islamic jurisprudence) books that are often used out of context, but rather a complete and comprehensive legal system and the spirit that enlivens it, such being the noble way of the Messenger of Allah, Allah bless him and give him peace. "You have indeed in the Messenger of Allah a beautiful pattern (of conduct) for anyone whose hope is in Allah and the Final Day, and who engages much in the praise of Allah" (Qur'an, 33:21).

The more fully we can apply the Sacred Law in our lives and emulate the Prophetic example, the richer our spiritual life and marriage will be. Good conduct is that which conforms to the example of the Messenger of Allah, Allah bless him and give him peace, as understood and practically interpreted by the Imams of Islamic law.

Everyone married must know the fiqh of marriage and divorce. Study them with a scholar or teacher from a reliable fiqh book from one of the schools of Sacred Law. If this is not possible, for a reliable source in English, you should read and become familiar with Book M (Book of Marriage) and Book N (Book of Divorce) from the *Reliance of the Traveller*. You should consult a scholar about any questions of fiqh.

The Sacred Law has to be the absolute basis of your married life: as a couple, you seek to implement it, encourage each other to perfect your observance of it, and resolve your problems according to it. As believers seeking to draw closer to Allah, you must exalt His commands and not transgress them. You should seek to become a person whose whole life is lived according to the Sacred Law. If you strive to do this, your marriage is bound to be stable, particularly as each partner will then be eager to obey Allah and to submit to His command.

"Allah loves those who shun transgressions and indecencies, and who forgive whenever they get angry" (Qur'an, 42:37). This is the word of Allah Almighty and Prophetic example we are expected to emulate. Though you will stumble, and there will be problems in your marriage, keep your objectives in sight, and seek to behave as the Prophet, Allah bless him and give him peace, would have in your situation, as Allah praises the behavior and character of His Messenger, Allah bless him and give him peace: "Verily, you are of an exalted standard of character" (Qur'an, 68:4). For you, it is mind over matter, will over habit.

As a serious Muslim, if you lack some good qualities you can develop them; just as you can rid yourself of bad or unpleasant ones because you are only what you decide to be. One's character is made by choice or indecision, either way you are responsible. The first step in breaking and overcoming a bad habit is to acknowledge and understand it. Think about your behavior. What percentage of it emanates from habit, and what percentage is rooted in intelligent choice? Often bad habits that seem impossible to change are so only because you have become resigned to them; in other words, you have let your nafs win.

Establishing good habits also requires acknowledgement and understanding with just as much effort on the nafs. Perhaps making a list of the ways or habits you do not like or want to be will help you in developing the 'likes' or 'wants' you choose to be daily. Bad habits that are easy to keep can often ruin your life. At first what seems difficult to change or develop with practice can positively transform your life.

The beginning of marriage offers a fresh context for establishing these new good habits. Marital happiness does not happen to you; rather, it is the result of the positive habits you have made and nurtured. If you do not make the effort to create and develop good habits, then what consequently develops is negative. There is no 'neutral' in marriage; it is either good or bad. The choice is yours. No one but you will live your life and what you make of it. However, you do need to realize that if you have children, they are affected by your choices just as much or even more than you are. Is there a thornless rose?

Either you are moving towards Allah and His pleasure or not. "O you who believe, turn sincerely to Allah from your own passions so that He may pardon your past evil-doings and cause you to enter paradise in the hereafter" (Qur'an, 66:8). Will your end be Allah's pleasure or the domination of your nafs?

Rumi wrote in his *Mathnawi*: "Self-control is the thing desired by the intelligent; sweetmeat is what children long for. Whoever practices self-control ascends to Heaven, whoever eats sweetmeat falls farther behind."

So have a broad viewpoint; see things as being sent from Allah and a means of drawing closer to Him. Do not think the blows of fate are separated from Allah's mercy and wisdom. If we are wise, we learn what we are supposed to learn from these trails. In every situation, think of how to be pleasing to Allah. Allah Most High says: "And He is Allah in the heavens and on earth. He knows what you hide and what you reveal, and He knows what you earn by your deeds" (Qur'an, 6:3).

The Messenger of Allah, Allah bless him and give him peace, said: "Fear Allah wherever you are, and follow a bad deed with a good one and it will wipe it out, and behave well towards people" (Tirmidhi, 1987). As seen in this and previous hadiths, your spouse is entitled to your best behavior if you obey Allah and His Messenger, Allah bless him and give him peace. So, do not let the devil fool you, you need not look right or left, these words are meant for you and not someone else.

The Wise Husband

*A*LLAH MIGHTY AND MAJESTIC guides the believers to the ways that please Him. The following verses are some of what He says:

- "But the best of provisions is right conduct. So fear Me, O you who are wise" (Qur'an, 2:197).

- "Those who spend (freely), whether in prosperity, or in adversity; who restrain anger, and pardon (all) men; for Allah loves those who do good" (Qur'an, 3:134).

- "Do men think that they will be left alone on saying, 'We believe', and that they will not be tested?" (Qur'an, 29:2).

- "And fear a day wherein you shall be returned to Allah, and every soul shall be paid in full what it earned" (Qur'an, 2:281).

Some men lack gentleness, and this manifests itself in an unconscious lack of compassion and affection towards their wives. That is why the Messenger of Allah, Allah bless him and give him peace, gave them much advice on the subject. He, Allah bless him and give him peace, said, "The believer who has the most exemplary faith is he who is best in demeanor and most kind to his wife" (Tirmidhi, 1162). A scholar explained, this hadith also means that the worst of you are those who are bad to their wives.

At the Farewell Pilgrimage, our beloved Prophet, Allah bless him and give him peace, said, "O men, listen to me, for I may not be with you after this year in this place. Let it be well understood that your lives and property are sacred and inviolable to each other. .... You have rights over your wives, they have rights over you... and all Muslims are brothers to one another. I call upon you all to guard yourselves against committing any injustice.... Listen! Treat women kindly; they are a trust for safe keeping in your hands" (Tirmidhi, 3087).

Allah Most High has said: "O you who believe! Stand out firmly for justice, as witnesses to Allah, even as against yourselves, or your parents, or your kin, and whether it be against rich or poor; Allah can best protect both. Follow not the lusts of your hearts, lest you swerve; if you distort or decline justice, verily Allah is well acquainted with all that you do" (Qur'an, 4:135).

Thus, the wise will take heed and control his nafs (ego) for the sake of Allah and live piously with his wife as Allah Mighty and Majestic and His Messenger, Allah bless him and give him peace, have commanded.

Love and Comfort

THE RELATIONSHIP OF COMFORT and support between husband and wife is mutual. "And (have We not) created you in pairs" (Qur'an, 78:8). Allah created human beings as social creatures, innately loving and needing love. The sexes were created to fulfill this need. Women were given the disposition to make and maintain the loving atmosphere of their home, and men were created as supportive protectors and thoughtful companions and providers.

As a practical example, a husband returning home should be greeted warmly. A wise wife maintains an affectionate, tender, physical relationship with her husband that should not make her feel shy or degraded. Allah has created women to be sensitive and emotional; this is their fitra (natural disposition).

It is necessary that both spouses feel responsible for expressing affection to the other. Consistency is the key. Remember if you want something, most often you first need to give it. Whenever you feel short of something, give what you want first and most likely, it will come back to you, e.g. a smile, friendship, love.

Likewise, the husband should come home greeting his wife with warmth and affection. Small gifts and surprises warm a relationship. It is good Islamic behavior to practice acts of kindness, random and planned. A husband bringing a gift, flowers or sweets to his wife, or doing an extra household chore, expresses a thoughtfulness that is difficult to go unappreciated. The Prophet, Allah bless him and give him peace, said that exchanging gifts increases love between people (al-Bayhaqi, 11726). Love pecks and cuddles are great gifts that any husband or wife can give, and in a healthy marriage, these should be abundant.

Caring and kindness make a comfortable resting place. Inability to properly fulfill emotional duties in marriage reflects remoteness from your fitra (true human nature). Accordingly, substantial effort is needed to overcome this remoteness in order to carry out the duty you have taken upon yourself through marriage as Allah Mighty and Majestic has demanded.

"O you who believe! Respond to Allah and His Messenger when He calls you to that which will give you life; and know that Allah stands between a man and his heart, and that to Him you shall be gathered. And fear tumult or oppression, which affects not in particular only the evildoers among you; and know that Allah is terrible in retribution" (Qur'an, 8:24-25).

Affection

"IT IS HE WHO CREATED you from a single person, and made his mate of like nature. In order that he might dwell with her (in love)" (Qur'an, 7:189).

Love is reciprocal. Frequent affectionate touching and tenderness that does not necessarily lead to sex is essential between the spouses. This type of intimacy on a daily basis is healthy for both spouses and consequential to the relationship, even if you find it difficult or consider it unnecessary. It may be because you find it difficult that you think it unnecessary.

To touch or be touched is a healthy and normal human need. Research shows that people deprived of physical contact are insecure, poorly adjusted and more prone to illness; infants actually die from the lack of it.

Though too much healthy love and attention is rarely a problem, too little is often a source of heartbreak. Expressing affection to your spouse is an indispensable form of worship that brings the family together in a wholesome Islamic atmosphere. "O you who believe, do your duty to Allah, seek the means of approach unto Him; and strive with might and main in His cause so that you may prosper" (Qur'an, 5:35).

Remember the family is the foundation of the Islamic community. Thus, it is under constant attack from shaytan and the nafs (lower self). These enemies will discourage any type of harmonious healthy relations. They regularly remind you of "all the wrongs" that have been done to you or anything that might make or keep you upset in order that love and kindness never develop between you and your spouse. They encourage this discord to ensure the lack of an affectionate and loving atmosphere at home in order to devastate the family, not necessarily by divorce, but by engendering a cold and sterile atmosphere, that perpetuates itself over the years.

Both partners naturally want and need affection and understanding. When this need is unmet, it sours the relationship. If left unresolved, this leads to frustration, disappointment, and eventually, rage, apathy or divorce: all of which are disasters.

Ask yourself, are you living as a single person with a roommate or as a married couple? Even if you do not mind living as a single person with a roommate, your spouse might. In that case, what options does the spouse looking for a married life have? Do not be surprised when that spouse starts probing into those options. If that bothers you, then you should realize that it is you who must keep your spouse satisfied.

Tenderness and the Female Nature (Fitra)

FOR WOMEN, sex is not necessarily an expression of love. It is essential that men understand that a wife needs to feel she is her husband's sweetheart and not merely a means for his sexual pleasure. This is not to say that she does not have a need for sexual fulfillment, but that consistent tenderness is usually equally important to a wife, and essential to the overall harmony of the marriage.

The wife's need for being a sweetheart often goes unnoticed by the husband, which makes it all the more heartbreaking for her and disastrous for the relationship. Taking care of your wife's emotional needs is an important step to getting your own needs fulfilled. The Prophet, Allah bless him and give him peace, said that diversions (lahw) are not permitted, except for in three cases, one of which is pleasantly spending time with your wife (Abu Dawud, 2513).

Some men's aversion to tenderness deprives the wife of her natural right and need. Should her husband make her doubt herself for wanting to love and be loved, he may drive her either to the unlawful, or to thinking that Islam is incomplete or to the perception that he does not love her, which in due course may lead to divorce. In reality, it is this husband who is deficient and failing to adhere to the command of Allah Most High and the orders and resplendent example of our beloved Prophet, Allah bless him and give him peace.

In the unusual case of it being the wife who is unaffectionate, she should fear Allah and remind herself of the duties He has commanded of her. Men are attracted to feminine not masculine women, and they marry to satisfy this need. Even if it is not her nature, she must make it so. Although her nafs (ego) might be deeply irritated by this, she should remember Allah's promise: "Verily, with every difficulty there is relief" (Qur'an, 94:6). It might help if she recalls the many Prophetic sayings, some of which have been previously mentioned in 'The Woman's Jihad' and 'The Wife Who Earns Paradise'.

If either the husband or the wife still finds it impossible to do this Islamic duty, then they need to reflect on whether they actually want to be a spouse or not. If they do not want to be married, then they should not be married because of the hurt their behavior causes to their spouse. Not being a proper spouse is a cause for Allah's displeasure, and the odds are that this occurs daily in some marriages.

"Not equal are the blind and those who (clearly) see: Nor are (equal) those who believe and work deeds of righteousness, and those who do evil. Little do you reflect"! (Qur'an, 40:58).

Bedroom Behavior

THE ROLE OF the sexual relationship and the problems that can arise from it are serious and should not be neglected. As difficult as it may seem, particularly for the newlywed, partners need to communicate any difficulties or anxieties in this area. This should be done with the utmost delicacy and tact. Establishing good habits in this sensitive facet of the marital relationship is essential.

One should know that it is haram (unlawful) to mention details of the sexual intimacy between you and your spouse to anyone, unless seeking advice, and even then, you should be as discrete as possible and discuss only that which is necessary. Once more, often people with good intentions impart bad advice. Thus, advice should be sought from those qualified to give it.

Desire

NEWLYWEDS MAY EXPERIENCE a high level of desire in the first months of their marriage. This is completely normal, healthy and to be expected. Marriage is the halal (lawful) outlet through which you can channel this desire. However, you should realize that the first months of marriage are not the norm. The first year is not like the second, and so on.

The gauge of whether you have exceeded what is considered moderate varies from person to person and from couple to couple. It is left to you as a couple to decide upon your mean; a mean with which you are both comfortable. If you both agree then whatever is suitable for you is acceptable. If you are beset by problems in terms of achieving this mean, you should formulate a plan with your spouse to solve it. As a couple, you need to work something out. To ignore or leave the problem unsolved is disastrous. You will expose your marriage to stress that will reverberate throughout the relationship, overtly and covertly; causing seemingly unrelated problems as well as endless tension to envelop the marriage. The disturbance and detrimental effects caused by this lack of harmony are serious and difficult to overcome if left unresolved.

Allah Most High loves fairness and moderation. If the problem is lack of gratification, then the husband must make the effort to satisfy his wife; if he is unable to by copulation then by other means of stimulation in order that her need is fulfilled. If the husband is unsatisfied then the wife may find other halal (permissible) means of satisfying him without her herself having to perform a ghusl (purificatory bath).

With some couples, you can find the husband excessive in his physical appetite at the expense of his wife's comfort and time. This is nonetheless his right and her duty, however, "Allah commands justice and the doing of good" (Qur'an, 16:90). A husband who is constantly seeking an intense sexual relationship with his wife must be aware that he is draining the energy that she needs to fulfill her other obligations. Moderation and consideration for the limitations of your spouse are to be foremost in the Muslim's mind when there is a difference in need. "O you who believe, make not unlawful the good things which Allah has made lawful for you, but commit no excess; for Allah loves not those given to excess" (Qur'an, 5:87). And Allah Mighty and Majestic continues to describe those given to excess: "Verily the squanders are brothers of the devils, and Satan is to his Lord ungrateful" (Qur'an, 17:27).

This can also be the case if the two are both actively seeking knowledge and marry one another expecting that their spouse will supportively recognize their struggle and act accordingly. In other words, a woman needs to be moderate materially and physically if she chooses to marry a student. A husband should understand that in marrying a student, it would naturally entail his forgoing some of his rights. He should be aware that these rights often extend beyond the bedroom and into the kitchen as well. If either partner agrees to forgo some of your rights, doing so is lawful, and you will be rewarded for your generosity and kindness. This all points out that, as a couple, you have to reach an agreement that you are both satisfied with or at least can manage with during this stage in your life.

When in doubt, remember Islam is the middle way and advises moderation in all things. Allah has declared, "Thus have We made of you a nation justly balanced, that you might be witnesses over the nations" (Qur'an, 2:143). As Muslim scholars say, "The best in all matters is moderation."

Sunnas of Intimate Contact

CERTAIN SUNNAS SHOULD be followed during the course of sexual intimacy. You should start with foreplay; sweet words and kissing as it may take a different amount of time for each spouse to become stimulated.

The Prophet, Allah bless him and give him peace, is reported to have said: "Do not approach your wife like an animal. Rather, send a messenger to her." They asked: "What is the messenger?" He replied: "Kissing and kind words" (Musnad al-Firdous).

The Messenger of Allah, Allah bless him and give him peace, is reported to have mentioned three shortcomings in a man, the third being that he approaches his wife and has intercourse before talking or being nice to her and finishes his need from her before she finishes her need from him (Musnad al-Firdous). This is a very serious unspoken problem among many.

Marriage in Islam should provide satisfaction for both the husband and the wife; and if someone is unwilling to do this, then they need to consider the injustice they are doing that most likely is occurring more often than not, and fear Allah Almighty.

Imam Ghazali in his *Ihya'* states that because a man gets gratification from his wife he should wait until she is also gratified from him. It may take time for her to get satisfied, but arousal without gratification may hurt her and this injustice can lead to anger and frustration and perhaps even reluctance and sin. A woman who is shy about expressing her pleasure may feel more comfortable if both partners are gratified simultaneously, while her husband is preoccupied with himself. Imam Ghazali advised, "One should make love to one's wife every four nights... (or) more or less than this, according to the amount she needs to remain chaste."

When having sexual intimacy, neither the head nor the feet of either spouse should face the direction of the qibla. Both partners should cover their nakedness from the Devil though not necessarily from each other. The Prophet, Allah bless him and give him peace, said, "If a man wants to be with his wife, let him cover himself because if he does not, the angels get shy and leave the Devil free to approach them" (Tirmidhi, 2800). This hadith shows it is permissible to be completely naked as long as you are covered with a sheet or something similar, otherwise the Devil advances.

Allah has granted the Devil a share in human offspring and money, when Allah's name is not mentioned at the outset. "Provoke those whom you can among them... mutually share with them wealth and children; and make promises to them. But the Devil promises them nothing but deceit" (Qur'an, 17:64).

Prior to intercourse, the following du'a (supplication) should be recited: Bismi Llâh, Allâhumma jannibnâ ash-shaytâna wa jannibi sh-shaytâna ma razaqtanâ. [In the name of Allah, O Allah, turn Satan from me, and turn Satan from what You bestow upon us.] The Prophet, Allah bless him and give him peace, said that if you conceive after making this supplication, the Devil will not be able to harm your child (Bukhari, 141).

When ejaculation is imminent, the man should say in his heart (without moving his tongue), Al-hamdulillâh al-ladhî khalaqa min al-ma'i basharan fa-ja'alahu nisaban wa sahran. [Praise be to Allah "Who has created man from water; then has He established relationships of lineage and marriage" (Qur'an, 25:54).]

It is offensive to stay in an impure state (janaba) for a long time. The Prophet, Allah bless him and give him peace, said, "Purification is not kept except by the believer" (Ibn Majah, 277). You should not leave home in a state of ritual impurity, as you cannot pray or recite the Qur'an in this state; and purity and cleanliness are the marks of the believer. The Messenger of Allah, Allah bless him and give him peace, said, "Purification is half of faith" (Muslim, 223).

If you have not performed a ghusl (purificatory bath) and want to eat or drink, it is the sunna to make ablution. Similarly, if you want to have sexual intercourse again, it is the sunna to wash your private parts and make ablution first. If the Prophet, Allah bless him and give him peace, was in the state of ritual impurity and wanted to eat or sleep, he would make ablution as for prayer (Muslim, 305). The Messenger of Allah, Allah bless him and give him peace, said that if someone makes love with his wife, then wishes to do so again, he should perform ablution between the two acts (Muslim, 308).

The Forbidden

ON THE COURSE of intimate contact, Allah Most High has made the vast majority of activities halal (lawful), with few prohibitions. Two things that are absolutely forbidden are approaching your wife while she is menstruating and sodomy.

The Prophet, Allah bless him and give him peace, said, "Whoever has intercourse with a woman during her menses or sodomizes a woman... has committed unbelief [if one considers any of theses permissible]" (Ibn Majah, 639).

Allah Most High says of menstruation: "They ask you concerning women's courses... keep away from women in their courses, and do not approach them until they are clean. But when they have purified themselves, you may approach them in that which Allah has ordained for you" (Qur'an, 2:222).

This does not prohibit physical affection during the monthly period altogether: only that which is between her navel and knees is unlawful lest it lead to copulation i.e. it is unlawful to touch the skin between the navel and the knees of your wife during her menses. The Prophet, Allah bless him and give him peace, when asked about approaching a wife in her menses, replied, "That which is above the izar (a wraparound that covers between the navel and knee); though to refrain is better" (Abu Dawud, 213). As well as saying, "Everything except actual intercourse" (Muslim, 302).

As for sodomy, it is one of the vilest and most despicable acts a man can commit. Anal intercourse is haram (unlawful) and cursed. Allah Most High says, "Your wives are a tillage for you; so approach your tillage as you will" (Qur'an, 2:223). Ibn 'Abbas explained the verse as meaning in any position; standing, sitting, front, or back but solely vaginal.

The Messenger of Allah, Allah bless him and give him peace, said, "Anal intercourse with one's wife is the lesser type of homosexuality" (Ahmad, 6667). "He who sodomizes a woman is accursed" (Ahmad, 9731). Furthermore, the Messenger of Allah, Allah bless him and give him peace, said, "Allah will not look at him [on the Judgment Day] who sodomizes his wife" (Ibn Majah, 1923).

In response to numerous inquiries on the topic of oral sex as it is practiced and understood in the West, the consensus among the sheikhs and traditional scholars is that it contravenes the adab (proper Islamic behavior) of an Islamic marriage, and is repulsive to a sound human nature (fitra). Although some argue that when married both partners become 'halal for each other from head to toe', oral sex remains contrary to the sunnas of sexual intimacy, as mentioned in the previous section. Also, one should note that the Hanafi school considers it haram to allow najasa (impurities) to enter one's mouth. Unfortunately, the wisdom behind many Islamic rulings is sometimes not fully appreciated by some until scientists discover detrimental health effects of behaviors that Allah in His Divine Wisdom has prohibited. For such people perhaps the recent studies highly suggestive of a particular strain of the HPV infection contracted through oral sex being a major risk factor in developing a certain type of mouth and throat cancer would be enough to remind them of the superior wisdom in the divinely decreed Islamic etiquette (see The New England Journal of Medicine Study: *Case–Control Study of Human Papillomavirus and Oropharyngeal Cancer*). When the actual details of oral sex have been described to traditional scholars, they plainly say it is haram (unlawful) and this should be sufficient for those who take heed. Those who abstain from questionable acts out of God-fearingness protect themselves and guard their faith.

The Question of Conception

*O*N THE MUSLIM WORLD, new couples are often expected to have a baby immediately. When people new to Islam marry, it is, in most cases, more advisable for them to postpone having a baby until they have adjusted to each other and are comfortably settled in their marriage. If you plan to wait, then get professional advice about your options. Factors will vary from couple to couple. Weigh the advantages and disadvantages; then choose the contraceptive method you both find suitable. Sterilization as a means of contraception is haram (unlawful) unless there is a medical need for it.

Children are a blessing from Allah Mighty and Majestic and if you plan to have a child, it is your duty to educate yourself on the matter beforehand. Having a baby often proves to be more demanding than most couples expect. Therefore, appropriate preparation helps. Having and raising a child is a serious responsibility that must be done properly because you will be asked about it on the Day of Judgment, if not before then.

Children affect and are affected by the state of their parents' marriage. If you want them to be good Muslims then it is essential that they see Islam working for you in your daily life. They must see you applying and loving Islam. A parent that half-heartedly applies Islam can hardly choose how much of Islam their kids will apply.

In this age, parents need to be creative or have religious, creative friends. Islam must be more than a religion of prohibitions for children; rather, it should be based on knowing and loving Allah Most Merciful. When they know and love their Creator, then following His rules will come easily. However, if they know nothing of their Lord, then following His rules becomes a meaningless burden. The extra amount of work that needs to be done depends on what type of environment the children are raised in and the personality of each child. It is the right of each child to have an Islamic upbringing; no one raises themselves. You should take this duty to heart before you are taken to task.

5

Divorce

A solution when all else fails

ALLAH MOST HIGH SAYS: "When you divorce women, divorce them at their prescribed periods. Count their prescribed periods, and fear Allah your Lord. Do not expel them from their houses, nor let them leave, except in case they are guilty of some open lewdness. Those are limits set by Allah; and any who transgresses the limits of Allah, does verily wrong his own soul. You do not know if perchance Allah will bring about thereafter some new situation" (Qur'an, 65:1).

Divorce is the most hated of halal (lawful) things (Abu Dawud, 2178). The throne of the All-merciful is said to shake at the divorce of a Muslim couple. Verily the family is the foundation of the Islamic society. Knowing that the Devil and the nafs (lower self) have numerous ways of causing discord, both spouses need to take sensible precautions. "They followed ...and they learned from them (the evil ones) the means to sow discord between man and wife..." (Qur'an, 2:102).

Patience, mercy and kindness can often work to solve many problems. Should difficult circumstances arise, remind yourself of the words of Allah Most High: "It was We who created man, and We know what dark suggestions his soul makes to him: For We are nearer to him than his jugular vein" (Qur'an, 50:16). Then ask yourself: How would the Prophet, Allah bless him and give him peace, have acted in this situation? As our actions and dealings with others are intended to be for Allah and to draw us nearer to Him, in times of distress, wonder: Is what I am doing drawing me closer to Allah? Again, before it becomes serious, discuss the problem. Allah Most Merciful advises: "If you fear a breach between the couple, appoint an arbiter from his people and from her people an arbiter; if they wish for peace, Allah will cause their reconciliation; surely Allah is All-knowing, All-aware" (Qur'an, 4:35).

Some men of hard hearts and low minds use the threat of divorce as a sword over the head of their wives to cow them into submission. Divorce, however, is meant as a last resort to an otherwise unsolvable situation. It is never intended to merely throw your weight around or prove your manhood.

We are responsible for everything we say, including pronouncements of divorce. It is such a dreaded thing that when studying fiqh (Islamic jurisprudence) with traditional sheikhs hesitate even to mention the word 'divorce' in the lesson. It is very tragic and often devastating when a man realizes that he has just ended his marriage 'with a word,' yearning to take it back but having no way to do so. The Messenger of Allah, Allah bless him and give him peace, said that there are three things that are always taken seriously even if said in jest: marriage, divorce and returning one's wife (Tirmidhi, 1184). And these are among the major reasons why those married must know the fiqh of divorce as well as marriage.

The Messenger of Allah, Allah bless him and give him peace, said: "A woman who asks her husband for divorce, when nothing is wrong, will not smell the perfume of paradise [be forbidden Paradise]" (Tirmidhi, 1187). Most sheikhs disapprove of divorce. Rather, they advise patience and counseling. Nevertheless, if you feel that divorce is your only option left, you should discuss it with proper Islamic manners.

Allah Most High says: "If a husband divorces his wife (irrevocably), he cannot remarry her after that until she has married another husband and he has divorced her. In that case there is no blame on either of them if they reunite, provided they feel that they can keep the limits ordained by Allah. Such are the limits ordained by Allah, which He makes plain to those who understand. When you divorce women, and they fulfill the term of their postmarital waiting period ('idda), then take them back on equitable terms or set them free on equitable terms; do not take them back to injure them, (or) to take undue advantage; whoever does that has wronged his own soul. Take not Allah's signs in mockery, but remember Allah's blessing on you, and the fact that He sent down to you the Book and Wisdom, for your instruction. And fear Allah, and know that Allah is well-acquainted with everything" (Qur'an, 2:230-1).

Should a husband divorce his wife irrevocably, he cannot take her back, that is remarry her, until she has married another, has consummated that marriage and is then divorced. In that case, they may remarry if they feel that they can keep the limits ordained by Allah.

"Divorce is twice; after that, the parties should either hold together on equitable terms or separate with kindness.

It is not lawful for you to take back any of your gifts from your wives, except when both parties fear that they would be unable to keep the limits ordained by Allah. If you fear that they would be unable to keep the limits ordained by Allah, there is no blame on either of them if she redeems herself. These are the limits ordained by Allah; do not transgress them. Whosoever transgresses the limits of Allah, those are the evildoers" (Qur'an, 2: 229).

Even while going through a divorce, we should behave as exemplary Muslims. Although this may seem difficult when you are under stress, remember that your good manners are for Allah, not for anything or anyone else. Allah has ordered us to live together on good terms and kindness or separate in the same manner.

"If a wife fears cruelty or desertion on her husband's part, there is no blame on them if they arrange an amicable settlement between themselves; and such settlement is best; even though men's souls are swayed by greed. But if you do good and practice self-restraint, Allah is well-acquainted with all that you do" (Qur'an, 4:128). This means if a wife no longer wishes to continue in the marriage, she may ask for a 'payment for a release from marriage' (khula').

When the divorcing couple does not come to an agreement concerning their children, they must both submit to the stipulations of the Sacred Law. As long as the mother remains unmarried, she keeps the children; the son until he can feed, dress, and go to the toilet unassisted (approximately seven years old), the daughter until she is nine years old. Thereafter they return to their father.

Lastly, divorce does not necessarily mean that one of the spouses is bad and the other good, or one right and the other wrong. Often they are both good, and right in a way, yet their differences and lack of understanding were too great for divorce to be avoided. Praise be to Allah Most Merciful, Most Wise; although divorce is extremely disliked, it remains a halal (lawful) last resort.

6

Merits of a Spiritual Marriage

Having gratitude to Allah

"AND ALLAH GAVE them a reward in this world, and the excellent reward of the Hereafter. For Allah loves those who do good" (Qur'an, 3:148).

This life is merely a means, and we, as people seeking closeness to Allah, strive to gather provisions on our way to the ultimate destination. A stable marriage is one of the greatest of these provisions. Marriage is training, discipline and a form of worship in its own right. Patient endurance of a spouse serves to train the soul, to subdue your hard-heartedness, and to improve your character.

When you live on your own, or keep agreeable company, the hidden vices of your soul do not rise to the surface, and inner faults remain hidden. By striving for a harmonious marriage, whoever travels the path to Allah is subjecting their nafs (ego) to various tests. Your character becomes balanced by learning to bear these patiently, your soul becomes disciplined, and your inner being purified of blameworthy qualities.

A traveler does not carry dead weight on his back, and a marriage for the sake of anything or anyone besides Allah Mighty and Majestic is of no use and will only be an obstacle. You should marry for His sake, be clement and gracious to your spouse for His sake, and restrain your nafs for His sake. Nothing you do for His sake is lost. Rumi wrote in his *Mathnawi*: "The soil is faithful to its trust, and whatever you have sown in it, you carry away the equivalent in kind thereof without fraud on the part of the soil. It has derived this faithfulness from that Divine faithfulness, inasmuch as the sun of Justice has shone upon it. Until springtime brings the token of Allah, the soil does not reveal its secrets."

Allah Most High has praised His awliya' (friends, the righteous) for requesting in their prayers, "Our Lord, grant us through our wives and our children a comfort to the eyes [stability and happiness through a good marriage] and make us a model to the God-fearing" (Qur'an, 25:74).

A harmonious marriage brings peace of mind, whereby the heart is free to be refreshed and strengthened in worship. The principal concern of a Muslim, aspiring to tread the path to the Allah, is to make his heart pure.

Finally, with the inevitable passage of time, marriage offers true comfort to the maturing couple who, having spent long years together worshipping and remembering Allah, can partake of the sweetness of what they have sown. Like many things, marriage is aged, and its flavor upon maturity depends largely on how it was maintained, and in what environment it was left to ripen over the years. A marriage replete with clemency and the love of Allah within hearts and bodies will ripen to a sweetness wherein the aging couple finds fulfillment and sanctuary, whether in sickness or in health. Such a state in the twilight of our lives offers an invaluable peace and haven. May it be one we all aspire to and strive to attain. And Allah Mighty and Majestic alone grants success.

"Allah will say: 'This is a day on which the truthful will profit from their truthfulness. Theirs are gardens, with rivers flowing beneath, their eternal home: Allah well-pleased with them, and they well-pleased with Him: that is the great salvation (the fulfillment of all desires)'" (Qur'an, 5:119).

Works Cited

'Abd al-Barr, Yusuf ibn 'Abd Allah. *al-Isti'ab fi ma'rifati al-Ashab*. 4 vols. Beirut: Dar al-Kutub al-'Ilmiyya, 1995.

Al-Abyani, Muhammad Zaid. *Sharh al-Ahkam al-Shar'iyya fi al-Ahwal al-Shakhsiyya*. 3 vols. Photocopy. Damascus, n.d.

'Ali, Abdullah Yusuf. *The Meaning of the Qur'an*. Brentwood: Amana Corp., 1991.

'Alwan, 'Abd Allah. *Tarbiyyatu al-Awlad fi al-Islam*. 2 vols. Beirut: Dar al-Fikr, 1996.

Arberry, A. J. *The Koran Interpreted*. 2 vols. New York: Simon and Schuster, 1996.

Al-Bayhaqi, Ahmad ibn al-Hussein. *Sunan al-Bayhaqi al-Kubra*. 10 vols. Mecca: Maktaba Dar al-Baz, 1994.

Al-Bazzar, Abu Bakr. *Al-Bahr al-Zakhkhar al-Ma'ruf bi Musnad al-Bazzar*. Ed. With notes by Mahfudh al-Raman Zayn Allah. 9 vols. [Incompete after vol. 9 due to editor's death.] Medina: Maktaba al-'Ulum wa al-Hikam, 1414/1993.

Al-Bukhari, Muhammad ibn Isma'il. *Sahih al-Bukhari*. 6 vols. Beirut: Dar Ibn Kathir, 1987.

Al-Daraqutni, Ali. *Sunan al-Daraqutni*. 4 vols. Beirut: Dar al-Ma'rifa, 1996.

Al-Ghazali, Abu Hamd Muhammad. *Ihya' 'ulum al-Din*. 4 vols. Cairo: Lejna nashr al-Thaqafa al-Islamiyya, 1935.

————. *Adab al-zawaj fi al-Islam*. Alexandria: Maktaba al-Sahaba, n.d.

Al-Hakam, Muhammad. *al-Mustadrak 'ala al-Sahihain*. 4 vols. Beirut: Dar al-Kutub al-'Ilmiyya, 1990.

Al-Idris, Mulana al-Tuhami. *Quratu al-'Uyun fi sharh nadham ibn Yamun fi al-Nikah al-Shar'i wa Adabihi*. Cairo: Mustafa al-Babi al-Halabi, 1982.

Al-Misri, Ahmad ibn Naqib, and Nuh Ha Mim Keller. *Reliance of the Traveller: A Classic Manual of Islamic Sacred Law*. Abu Dhabi: Modern Printing Press, 1991.

Al-Nasa'i, Abu 'Abd al-Rahman Ahmad. *al-Sunan al-Kubra*. 6 vols. Beirut: Dar al-Kutub al-'Ilmiyya, 1991.

Al-Nawawi, Yahya ibn Sharaf. *al-Arba'un al-Nawawiyya wa sharhuha*. Cairo: al-Maktaba al-Salafiyya, 1977.

————. *An-Nawawi's Forty Hadith*. Trans. Ezzeddin Ibrahim and Denys Johnson-Davies. Damascus: The Koran Publishing House, 1976.

Al-Quda'i, Muhammad ibn Salama. *Musnad al-Shihab*. 2 vols. Beirut: Mu'assasa al-Risala, 1986.

Al-Qanuji, Muhammad Saddiq. *Husn al-Uswat bi ma thabata min Allah wa rasulihi fi al-Niswa*. Beirut: Mu'assasa al-Risala, 1996.

Al-Sha'rani, 'Abd al-Wahhab Ahmad. *Lawaqih al-Anwar al-Qudsiyya fi bayan al-'Uhud al-Muhammadiyya*. Cairo: Mustafa al-Babi al-Halabi, 1973.

Al-Sijistani, Abu Dawud. *Sunan Abi Dawud*. 4 vols. Beirut: Dar al-Fikr, n.d.

Al-Suyuti, Jalal al-Din. *al-Jami' al-Saghir min hadith al-bashir al-nadhir*. 2 vols. Damascus: 'Abd Allah Muhammad Darwish, n.d.

Al-Tabarani, Sulaiman ibn Ahmad. *al-Mu'jam al-Awsat*. 2 vols. Riyadh: Maktaba al-Ma'arif, 1985.

———. *al-Mu'jam al-Kabir*. 20 vols. Mosul: Maktaba al-'Ulum wa al-Hikam, 1983.

———. *al-Mu'jam al-Saghir*. 2 vols. Beirut: al-Maktab al-Islami, 1985.

Al-Tirmidhi, Abu 'Isa Muhammad. *Sunan al-Tirmidhi*. 5 vols. Beirut: Dar Ihya' al-Turath al-'Arabi, n.d.

D'Souza, Gypsyamber, et al. *Case–Control Study of Human Papillomavirus and Oropharyngeal Cancer*. The New England Journal of Medicine Study, vol 356:1944-1956, no. 19 (May 10, 2007).

Ibn 'Abidin, Muhammad Amin. *Radd al-Muhtar 'ala al-Durr al-Mukhtar*. 6 vols. Beirut: Dar Ihya' al-Turath al-'Arabi, 1407/1987.

Ibn Hanbal, Ahmad. *Musnad al-Imam Ahmad*. 6 vols. Cairo: Mu'assasa Qurtuba, n.d.

Ibn Hibban, Muhammad. *Sahih Ibn Hibban*. 18 vols. Beirut: Mu'assasa al-Risala, 1993.

Ibn Kathir, Isma'il ibn 'Umar. *Tafsir al-Qur'an al-'Azim*. 4 vols. N.d. Reprint. Beirut: Dar al-Ma'rifa, 1983.

Ibn Majah, Muhammad. *Sunan ibn Majah*. 2 vols. Beirut: Dar al-Fikr, n.d.

Khin, Mustafa, Mustafa al-Bugha, Muhyiddin Misto, 'Ali al-Shirbaji, and Muhammad Lutfi. *Nuzha al-Mutaqin sharh Riyad al-Salihin*. 2 vols. Beirut: Mu'assasa al-Risala, 1988.

Muslim ibn al-Hajjaj. *Sahih Muslim*. 5 vols. Beirut: Dar Ihya' al-Turath al-'Arabi, 1954.

Nicholson, Reynold A. *The Mathnawi of Jalaluddin Rumi*. 3 vols. London: Luzac & Co. LTD., 1977.

Niffari, Abdul Jabar. *Spiritual Stations and Addresses*. Trans. A. J. Arberry. London: Gibb Memorial Trust Publications, 1935.

Özek, Ali and Nureddin Uzunoğlu, Tevfik Rüştü Topuzoğlu and Mehmet Maksutoğlu. *The Holy Qur'an with English Translation*. Istanbul: Acar Matbaacilik Yayincilik A.Ş., 2000.

About the Author

Hedaya Hartford is known for her Sacred Law expertise on women's issues regarding the fiqh of menstruation, lochia, marriage, divorce, and modern social issues. Born and raised in California, she graduated from the University of California, Berkeley. She entered Islam in 1981.

A teacher and translator, she currently lives with her husband Ashraf Muneeb in Amman, Jordan. She has written *Islamic Marriage*; and has co-authored with her husband *Your Islamic Marriage Contract*; a critical edition and commentary of *Risala al-Birgivi* in Arabic; and *Birgivi's Manual Interpreted: Complete Fiqh of Menstruation & Related Issues* in English.

By Hedaya Hartford and Ashraf Muneeb

BIRGIVI'S MANUAL INTERPRETED
Complete Fiqh of Menstruation and Related Issues

BIRGIVI'S MANUAL INTERPRETED is the explanative translation of a major Islamic legal work on menstruation, lochia, and related issues. The primary text, *Dhukhr al-Muta'ahhilin* by Imam al-Birgivi, is the most authoritative work on this topic in the Hanafi school, which the majority of Muslims follow. The work has been commentated upon by Imam Ibn 'Abidin, the central scholar of the late Hanafi school. Hedaya Hartford and Ashraf Muneeb have studied under various sheikhs, among them Sheikh Muhammad Amin Siraj of Turkey, a traditional Hanafi scholar who has an unbroken chain to Imam al-Birgivi himself. Sheikh Siraj gave Hartford and Muneeb his authorization to teach this volume in a written ijaza that attests, in his words, to their "full comprehension and meticulous understanding" of the work.

"A handbook of what a Muslim woman needs to know about her monthly period and related questions. The detailed content of this major work should make it useful for anyone teaching women's fiqh."

–Nuh Keller

"...explains the legal rulings related to menstruation and lochia in a clear and practical manner that enables women to fulfill their religious duties soundly, without the confusion and uncertainty that come from acting without knowledge."

–Faraz Rabbani, *Sunni Path*

By Hedaya Hartford and Ashraf Muneeb

YOUR ISLAMIC MARRIAGE CONTRACT

Men and women should have clear expectations in their marriage, and they should make a suitable Islamic contract to help facilitate their mutual goals. The main objectives of this booklet are to provide a variety of valid Islamic marriage contracts, to illustrate how to state conditions in a marriage contract, to explain the stringent conditions that must be present for a woman to marry without a wali (guardian), and to illustrate how the right of divorce can be given to the wife. Included are several contracts in attractive fonts, as well as one in Arabic.

"In their valuable and long overdue volume, *Your Islamic Marriage Contract*, Hedaya Hartford and Ashraf Muneeb address one of the greatest problems plaguing Muslims in the West; the lack of adequate, standardized wedding contracts. This problem leads to grave consequences including invalid divorces and marriages. By presenting the reader with a number of variously formatted forms, all written in consultation with one of the Muslim World's leading jurist-consults, Hartford and Muneeb go a long way in addressing such problems. This book will prove an indispensable aid to Imams and Community leaders in America and elsewhere in the West."

–Zaid Shakir